The Prayer Life of Jesus

David M. McIntyre

Christian Focus Publications

© 1992 Christian Focus Publications Ltd

ISBN 1 857 92 0 104

Scripture quotations are from
the Revised Version

Published by
Christian Focus Publications Ltd
Geanies House, Fearn, Ross-shire,
IV20 1TW, Scotland, Great Britain.

Cover design
by
Seoris N. McGillivray.

Printed and bound in Great Britain by
Cox & Wyman Ltd, Reading

CONTENTS

Christian Focus Publications
also publish

The Hidden Life of Prayer

by

David M. MacIntyre

A book which stimulates our prayer-life by
looking at Scripture teaching illustrated by
examples from biblical and Church history.

pocket paperback

ISBN 1 871 676 258   96 pages

CHAPTER ONE

INTRODUCTION

As prayer is the most exalted experience of which the mind of man is capable, so it is the least patient of analysis. The manner in which the Spirit of God acts upon the human spirit must ever remain a mystery. For ourselves, we have not made much progress in the exercise of prayer, if we are not acutely sensible of the insistence of desires so vast and formless that they fail to convey a distinct image to the mind: at such times our supplications express themselves only in groanings that cannot be uttered. Nor shall we be able rightly to estimate the prayer-life of another, until we have first sounded the depths of his personality, our insight piercing to the dividing of soul and spirit. How impossible, then, must it be for us to speak worthily of our Saviour's intercession! The secret of his wondrous Person is treasured and safeguarded in his life of prayer, but it is revealed as yet only in part, for 'no one knoweth the Son save the Father'.

Our Lord entered into creaturehood, and was manifested in the likeness of sinful flesh. He was born under law; he bowed with submission before the divine will. His spiritual life was nourished, as ours is, by the means of grace. As the Son of Man he preserved communion with the Father through prayer. We are privileged from time to time to overhear his priestly utterances before God; but we are rarely admitted into the oratory where his private requests were offered. Such joyous intimacy, such earnestness, such filial reverence as were displayed in those high communings with the Unseen, must far transcend our narrow experience. Never man prayed like this Man.

In one important particular the prayers of the Lord were unlike those of other men. He who knew no sin, but always did the things that pleased the Father, had no confession of unworthiness to offer to God. His was 'the only conscience without a scar'. There could, therefore, be no bar to communion with the Holy One, no distance required to be surmounted, no way of access had to be devised and secured. At the close of his earthly life, he lifted up to the Father for acceptance the full tale of his sinless years, saying:

'I glorified thee on the earth, having accomplished the work which thou hast given me to do. And now, O Father, glorify thou me with thine own self' (John 17: 4-5).

The prayers of the Lord Jesus, though little is said of this in Scripture, must have been radiant with thanksgiving. Even in that dark hour when

Capernaum, his own city, rejected him, he rejoiced in the Holy Spirit, and said:

> 'I thank thee, O Father, Lord of heaven and earth, that thou didst hide these things from the wise and understanding, and didst reveal them unto babes: yea, Father, for so it was well-pleasing in thy sight' (Luke 10:21).

His grateful devotion pierced the clouds, and poured forth under the blue heavens a song of adoring praise, sweeter than the hymns of angels. Even when he stood within one hour of Gethsemane's agony, within a day of Calvary's thick darkness, he testified to the buoyancy of his spirit:

> 'Now I come to thee; and these things I speak in the world, that they may have my joy fulfilled in themselves' (John 17:13).

And the disciples understood; they knew that there was no happier man in Jerusalem that night than he who was thus anointed with the oil of gladness above his fellows.

We cannot doubt that much of the Saviour's engagement with heaven in his hours of solitary prayer was in the communion of holy love with the Father. On the mountain-edge there was, we may believe, a nightly renewal of that fellowship which is beyond knowledge, an interchange of affection which the Incarnation had not weak-

ened, though it had lessened its sweet immediacy. So that, mingling with the ineffable repose
of the Son in the bosom of the Father, there ran
the strain of eager longing which was to find its
full expression in the High-Priestly Prayer:

'And now, O Father, glorify thou me with thine
own self with the glory which I had with thee
before the world was... for thou lovedst me before
the foundation of the world' (John 17:5-24).

The Son of Man dwelt ever in the presence of
God; and yet, in the days of his flesh, he yearned
for that glad hour when, having completed his
redemptive toil, he should ascend from his vol-
untary humiliation to the Uncreated Glory, and,
bringing our manhood with him, resume his Ses-
sion in God.

We must not, however, suppose that the
prayers of the Lord were only thanksgiving and
adoration. He had many requests to offer, in
supplication and intercession.

He prayed for his disciples - for their escape
from temptation (Luke 22:32), for the success of
their labours (Luke 10:18), for their advancement in holiness and love (John 17:11).

He prayed for those who were still strangers
to his grace - the world of men (John 17:21, 23),
the tribes of the House of Israel (Luke 10:2), the
rebellious children of Jerusalem, to whom he
had stretched out his hands, no man regarding

(Luke 19:42; Matt 23:37), the soldiers who pierced his hands and feet (Luke 23:34).

And for himself he prayed - for guidance in the crises of his life (Luke 6:12), for the continued supply of power in the prosecution of his ministry (Luke 11:1), for life to be granted at his word to Lazarus lying dead (John 11:41); that, if it were possible, the bitter cup might pass from him (Matt 26:39), or, failing this, that the will of his Father might be fully wrought (verse 42).

'I know that thou hearest me always,' (John 11:42) said the Saviour at the tomb of Lazarus. All his prayers were answered. But it must be remembered that there were petitions which he refused to offer. In the ignominy of his arrest he said to Simon:

> 'Thinkest thou that I cannot beseech my Father and he shall even now send me more than twelve legions of angels? How then should the Scriptures be fulfilled, that thus it must be?' (Matt 26:53-54).

He would not ask to be delivered from the hands of men. Not many days before, anticipation of the agony that was so soon to fall had forced from him the cry:

> 'Now is my soul troubled, and what shall I say?' Shall I say, 'Father, save me from this hour? But for this cause came I unto this hour. Father, glorify thy name' (John 12:27-28).

He will not offer prayer except within the will of God. And so long as that will has not been fully revealed, his requests are tendered with submissiveness: 'Not my will, but thine, be done' (Luke 22:42).

His prayers were always heard, but the answer did not always come at once. God, it has been said, has his seasons and delays; even the Son must wait upon the divine wisdom.

The Lord Jesus prayed that Israel might repent and turn to the Lord, but for two thousand years the Chosen Race has been wandering in the wilderness. He prayed that the nations should be given to him for an inheritance and the uttermost parts of the earth to be his possession, but to this hour 'the whole world lieth in the evil one'.

Nevertheless, it is written that the rejectors of the Messiah shall one day look on him whom they have pierced, and mourn. And for our sad, sin-cursed earth, the day is drawing near when the kingdom of the world shall become the kingdom of our Lord and of his Christ, and he shall reign for ever and ever.

As we have indicated, those prayers of Christ which are referred to in the Gospels are for the most part concerned with his mediatorial work. The Surety claims for his people the fullness of the divine mercy; the Good Shepherd makes intercession for the flock which he is about to purchase with his blood.

Accordingly, so far as the record informs us, our Lord's engagements in prayer, with scarcely an exception, gather round that act of allegiance to the will of God by which the Redeemer bowed himself under the curse, assuming our sin as his own. Let us note these instances among others: his Baptism, his Temptation, his Preparation for the Calling of the Twelve, his Supplication after the Feeding of the Five Thousand, the High-Priestly Prayer, the Agony in the Garden, and the Voices of his Passion.

All these have Golgotha in view; they are the disclosure to us of what death meant to Christ. To the Saviour the mere article of dissolution could only prove to be the striking off of earthly fetters and the return to the Right Hand of power. Nor could the fierce aspect of the torturing cross terrify this Man, most fearless of all who have looked with unflinching eyes on pain. His royal spirit made him in this, as in all else, more than conqueror.

But the death that occupied his waking thoughts, and became the predominant theme of his supplications, until he came to 'inhabit his passion', was such a death as no son of Adam had ever undergone. Countless millions have paid the debt to nature, but our blessed Lord *tasted death* for every man. 'It is Christ that died.' The prayers of Jesus are written red in the blood of sacrifice. And so they reveal to us, as no other words have done, what the Cross signified to him who passed his earthly life under its benign but awful shadow.

The writer of the Epistle to the Hebrews tells us that our Lord 'learned obedience by the things which he suffered', and associates this discipline with the exercise of prayer: 'He offered up prayers and supplications with strong crying and tears' (Heb 5:7-8). These words recall to our minds the agony in the Garden, but perhaps they have a wider reference. Not only upon Olivet, but often elsewhere, our Lord may have been plunged into anguish and amazement. On such occasions his refuge was the audience-chamber of God. And there, in the divine embrace, he became perfect through suffering (Heb 2:10; 5:8). In many of the Psalms and in the Prophetic Word the sorrows of the saints seem to mirror the experience of the Master:

'Out of the depths have I cried unto thee, O Lord... I wait for the Lord, my soul doth wait, and in his word do I hope. My soul looketh for the Lord, more than the watchmen look for the morning' (Psalm 130:1-6)

The intensity of the prayers of the Saviour was equalled only by the unconquerable faith in which they were presented to the Father. The word of encouragement to the ruler of the synagogue, 'Fear not; only believe,' must often have been addressed to his own spirit. It was, no doubt, out of his own experience that he spoke, when he laid on his disciples the supreme condition of their acceptable approach to the Father:

'Have faith in God. Verily I say unto you, Whosoever shall say unto this mountain, Be thou taken up, and cast into the sea; and shall not doubt in his heart, but shall believe that what he saith cometh to pass; he shall have it. Therefore I say unto you. All things whatsoever ye pray and ask for, believe that ye have received them, and ye shall have them' (Mark 11:22-24).

He confronted apparent disaster with undoubting heart; in desertion and forsakenness he comforted himself with the thought: 'The Father is with me.' He embraced the cross, pillowing his dying head upon the ordered covenant. His enemies, gathering round the tortured Son of God, bore witness to the most patent feature of his holy character: 'He trusteth on God' (Matt 27:43). They marked that then, in that dread hour, his confidence in the Eternal Love was undimmed.

Ere his ministry drew to a close our Lord antedated his passion, and prepared to enter on that heavenly priesthood which had awaited him from the first of time.

'Father,' he exclaims, 'that which thou hast given me, I will that, where I am, they also may be with me; that they may behold my glory, which thou hast given me: for thou lovedst me before the foundation of the world' (John 17:24).

This is not the plea of suffering manhood; it is a request by One who holds the right of intervention on behalf of his tried and afflicted people. This heavenly ministry our High Priest shall exercise till the end of all the ages, for he liveth to make intercession for us. And his advocacy is for ever presented in the power of an accepted Sacrifice.

CHAPTER TWO

THE HOLY CHILD

Our Lord Jesus was nurtured in a home in which prayer was a habitual exercise. The spirit of devotion presided over all the household arrangements, and every duty of the day was jewelled with acts of worship. If it be true that 'Prayer is the simplest form of speech that infant lips can try,' we shall not be able to date the beginning of our Lord's prayer-life. In his earliest childhood his mother would recite to him many of the Hebrew Psalms, to this day the fountains of our purest devotion. Joseph would carefully impress upon him the first and greatest precept of the law: 'Thou shalt love the Lord thy God with all thine heart, and with all thy soul, and with all thy might'; and love would certainly find expression in communion with the Beloved.

As soon as the young child had learned letters, the Sacred Writings were placed in his hand. As he bent over the parchments, heaven would open above him, and he would be at rest in the home of God. We may be sure that in youth, as in later years, his every thought turned heavenward, his every word was spoken in the audience of the Father. There would also be with the boy Jesus, as with other Hebrew children, a cheerful observance of the ritual of the day; he would pass through ordered seasons of prayer, public and private.

We may let our imagination linger over the spiritual exercises of the Holy Child, but where Scripture is silent we must refrain from speech. It is perhaps impossible for us to understand the unfolding of a spirit innocent of sin and supremely recipient of God.

The one flower plucked from the garden of that blameless childhood speaks to us of a tender intimacy existing between Jesus and his heavenly Father, and seems to imply a heightening of spiritual experience. That we are not too bold in suggesting this appears in the words written in the Gospel of the Infancy, probably by the mother's hand:

'Jesus advanced in wisdom and stature, and in favour with God and men' (Luke 2:52).

He had, with a devout humility, been anticipating his entrance on the full privileges of covenant sonship with Jehovah, the God of Israel. The emotions which stir the heart of a Christian youth, who is looking forward to his first public profession of faith at the Table of the Lord, may help us, if only in a limited measure, to understand the prayerful desire which filled the mind of Jesus as he addressed himself to meet the solemn obligations that were imposed on one who should become a son of the law. Nor did he refuse to make a confidante of his mother. His filial remonstrance, when his mother breathlessly rebuked him, leads us to infer that she ought to have remembered the sacred revealings of his heart disclosed to her in the Nazareth home, when the Passover festival was drawing night: 'How is it that ye sought me? Wist ye not that I must be in my Father's house?'

Now we may think of the Youth whose schooldays are ended, and who has been apprenticed to the trade of carpenter and builder. He would join not only in the worship of the home, but also in the prayers of the synagogue, breathing into them, without doubt, a deeper meaning than that which lay in the mere letter of the word, as he supplicated Heaven's mercy, not only on his fellow-townsmen of Nazareth, but on all the people of Israel and on the Seventy Nations beyond.

During those years our Lord acquired a remarkable familiarity with the ancient Scriptures. In the cottage of Joseph the carpenter - himself a son of David, there would probably be found some of the sacred scrolls - Deuteronomy, the Psalms, Isaiah, perhaps, if we may draw any conclusion from the frequent appeal which the Lord Jesus made to these books. For some of the other Holy Writings he may have been dependent on the synagogue chest. Nor can we think of his study of his Father's word - for such it was to him - without picturing to ourselves the continual uprising of his thoughts toward that Holy One whom the open scroll revealed.

Our Lord's study of the Scriptures must have been inwrought, like some costly mosaic, with praise and adoration, petition and intercession. He would inlay every commandment in renewed consecration, every promise in heartfelt acceptance, every disclosure of the divine character in thanksgiving. Each separate word of God would be wrought by prayer into the framework of his life.

That there were special times of prayer, quiet hours of waiting upon God, when the youthful Carpenter of Nazareth withdrew from his fellows and from his tasks, and sought in solitude the face of his Father, we may be sure - not merely from our sense of what is fitting and needful, but also from our Lord's practice in the days of his ministry. Then, he continually sought the mountain silences. In Nazareth, he may often have climbed the hill that rises above the village, that he might be alone with God; more often, perhaps, he entered into the 'closet' the little store-room tucked in between the living-room and the workshop. Is there not a touch of reminiscence in these words?

'Thou, when thou prayest, enter into thine inner chamber, and having shut they door, pray to thy Father which is in secret, and thy Father which seeth in secret, shall recompense thee' (Matt 6:6).

It is good for us to remember this. A zealous labourer in the kingdom of God may say: 'I am too busy to spend much time in prayer; and 'work, you know, is prayer'. Another, occupying a different standpoint, may profess: 'I am praying all day long; I do not need to observe set seasons; my entire life is one of intercourse with Heaven.' But we have not so learned Christ. No one was so careful to buy up the opportunity as he, no one maintained so heavenly a poise of spirit, yet the hours hastened while he prayed.

The experience of all saints is clear upon this - that we must carve out of the busiest day a quiet space in which we shall be silent before God. We must summon ourselves before the divine tribunal, permitting the light of God to stream in upon us, searching every motive, bringing every hidden thing to light, granting to us a fresh sense of pardon and acceptance, and revealing in new and ever more glorious aspects the divine holiness. So shall there be wrought in us the spirit of grace and of supplications. And God, even our own God, shall bless us.

CHAPTER THREE

ON THE THRESHOLD OF HIS MINISTRY

From Malachi, until the advent of John the son of Zacharias, there were in Israel moralists and historians, psalmists and seers, but no prophet. For centuries men had been asking for an immediate utterance of God, but the voice of prophecy was silent.

John was in the deserts until the day of his showing unto Israel. We may suppose that, as he dwelt in his father's house in the hill country of Judaea, the burden of the nation's guilt oppressed him. It was a time of spiritual darkness; the maxims of the age were worldly, and the practice of the people was ungodly. John fled from contamination as from a pestilence: he had 'known pureness from a child', and the very touch of sin pained him. He left behind him the voices of earth, and in the solitary places of the desert prayed: 'Speak, Lord; thy servant heareth.'

Then 'the word of the Lord came unto John the son of Zacharias in the wilderness.' And with the word power was given. He returned to the haunts of men, clad in the investiture of the Spirit. His message was that which had been spoken by the prophets of the olden time, soon to be caught up afresh and proclaimed by our Lord and his apostles: 'Repent, and believe the Gospel' - the eternal announcement of the divine mercy. 'Then went out unto him Jerusalem, and all Judaea, and all the region round about Jordan.' Soldiers of Rome, tax-gatherers, vine-dressers, and fishermen - all the best in Israel, and all the worst - were there. Many of the Pharisees and Sadducees came in curiosity, but they did not submit to the baptism of John.

1

Baptism was an ancient rite in Israel, and it had been employed in later years to seal the admission of Gentile proselytes to the household of promise. The new feature of this ceremony in the hands of John was that it was administered to Israel. A proselyte was said to be 'newborn' when he submitted to the ordinance of baptism; so that in this rite John is saying to priest and scribe, 'Ye must be born again.'

But if the official classes of religious Israelites refused to humble themselves in submission to the baptism of repentance, a Greater than they stooped to receive it: 'Then cometh Jesus to the Jordan unto John, to be baptised of him.' All the postulants for baptism, until now, had come confessing sin. Jesus came in the way of righteousness (cf.: Matt: 3:15). He had no sin to confess; why, then, did he take the place of a sinner?

In his incarnation he entered our nature, taking our liabilities upon himself. Our Kinsman Redeemer, he came to be our Surety and Substitute. And now, as he is set apart for his Messianic ministry, he joins himself to the communion of sinners, accepting baptism in waters that had borne away the guilt of an ungodly nation. In an act of humiliation, to be perfected only on the cross, he unites himself with the fallen race.

This, in his covenant relation to his people.

Personally, however, his baptism was his self-consecration to the duties of the august service which he had undertaken.

'Now it came to pass, when all the people were baptised, that Jesus also having been baptised and praying, the heaven was opened, and the Holy Ghost descended in a bodily form, as a dove, upon him, and a voice came out of heaven, Thou art my beloved Son; in thee I am well pleased' (Luke 3:21-22).

The decisive step has been taken, the ordinance which ratified the momentous transaction has been administered, and now Jesus gives himself to prayer. In this prayer, as we may believe, all the motives and purposes which gather round the solemn act of his baptism find expression.

(a) He accepts the commission entrusted to him. He arrays himself in the mantle of the Messiah - Jesus is now the Christ. All the Scriptures have foretold his coming and declared his mighty acts. And not as the Christ only: he is proclaimed to be God's very Son. As in eternity he received from the Father a multitude of lost souls and engaged to die for them; so, in the inauguration of his earthly ministry, in human weakness and under the shadow of death, he renews the high, eternal covenant in God.

(b) He offers himself as the propitiation for the sins of a lost world. The voice from the opened heavens, 'This is my beloved Son, in whom I am well pleased,' is reminiscent of the Isaianic prophecy of the Servant of Jehovah (cf.: Isa 42:1). For such an announcement there must have been a preparedness in the mind of Christ. The voice came out of heaven, but it was responded to in the depths of our Lord's consciousness. The Servant foretold was Israel's Messiah, predestined to suffer. It was of him that the epitaph was inscribed by the Father, as on the rock-hewn tomb:

> 'He poured out his soul unto death,
> And was numbered with the transgressors:
> Yet he bare the sin of many,
> And maketh intercession for the transgressors.'

This Sufferer is now declared from heaven to be none other than Jesus the Nazarene, and the young Prophet of Galilee girds himself for his passion. A path of thorns, with a cross at the end of the way, this our Lord in Jordan prayerfully enters upon.

(c) He asks for himself a sufficiency of grace and strength - that he may have 'an honourable through-bearing'. Now the Spirit descends to dwell with the sinless One; the Lord of the house has come to his temple, saying: 'This is my rest for ever: here will I stay; for I have desired it.' This advent of the Spirit, however, is only the completion of a uniting act prolonged over thirty years. Our Lord Jesus was Spirit-born (Luke 1:35), Spirit-taught (Isa 11:2), Spirit-engraced (Isa 61:1); from this hour, in an especial manner, he is Spirit-empowered.

The mystery of the descent of the Spirit upon the Son lies hidden in the depths of the Divine Nature; yet is partly revealed in the Incarnation of the Word, for the Spirit of God is the bond of union between the dual elements in the Person of Christ. But, as it behoved him to be made in all things like unto his brethren, we may gather from our narrow experience something of what the donation of the Spirit at Jordan must have meant to our Saviour.

A minister who is being inducted into the pastoral charge of a congregation, a missionary who is being set apart for foreign service, asks for, and by faith receives, the enduement of power from on high. The gifts bestowed are adequate to the necessities of the work entrusted to him. He puts on the robe of strength, even as our Lord has said (Luke 24:49). But the endowment which the Saviour craved was that sovereign gift of power which would enable him to bear away the sins of the world, destroy the works of the devil, dethrone the evil one who had usurped dominion, make an end of sin, and open the gates of life to all who should believe. He asked, and all power in heaven and on earth was placed at his disposal. But the power came with (and in) the Spirit. By the Spirit he cast out devils, by the Spirit he gave commandment unto the apostles whom he had chosen, and by the Eternal Spirit he offered himself unto God as a 'perfect redemption, propitiation, and satisfaction' for the sins of the whole world.

2

In the story of the Temptation, related, one cannot doubt, by our Lord himself, there is no mention of prayer. But the forty days' fast surely implies, and the parallelism of the temptation in the Wilderness with the agony in the Garden does at least suggest, that it was in a protracted season of supplication, which left a wanness as of death on our Lord's countenance (cf.: John 1:29) and drew to him a band of ministering angels, that the victory over the tempter was won.

The temptations which beset our Lord during the forty days of fasting are not recorded. But the

triple assault which closed the series, and perhaps summed up the evil solicitations endured in
this prolonged retreat, has been made known to
us. The point of each of these last incitements of
the tempter was that the Messiah should shun
the predestined sorrow, and evade the way of the
cross. 'Master, pity thyself.'

(a) The first assault of this closing hour was an
appeal to the principle of self-preservation: 'If
thou be the Son of God, command that these
stones become bread' (Matt 4:3).

This is, in a more impellent form, the temptation before which our first parents fell. They
were tempted in the Garden of delights, he in the
Wilderness where wild beasts were his only companions.

They had all that heart could wish, except the
right to partake of one seductive but deleterious
fruit: he was faint with hunger and near to death.
And with him, as with them, the way for the
entrance of temptation into the mind was prepared by the suggested doubt of the Father's
love and truth. 'If thou be the Son of God.' He
has affirmed it, but is it true? And if true, where
is the Father's care? Act independently. Provide
for thyself. Command these stones that they
become bread.

Where exactly did the sinfulness of such a
suggestion lie? It meant retractation of the Incarnation. He had entered into our nature, that

he might live a holy life and die an atoning death in our proper manhood, living his life within the modes of our common humanity. It is true that he was God's co-essential Son, but it was not given him to draw upon the resources of his divine nature. To draw upon them now would be to renounce his solidarity with the race.

And as his coming into our manhood was by the decree and council of God, to reverse the great humiliation of his entrance into manhood would be to disobey that holy will to which he was always subject, and (if that were possible) to introduce discord into the Being of God. The principle of our Lord's activity as the Incarnate Word is thus stated by himself:

> 'The Son can do nothing of himself, but what he seeth the Father doing; for what things soever he doeth, these the Son also doeth in like manner' (John 5:19).

(b) The second assault of the evil one according to the report given in the First Gospel - and this appears to be the natural order - passes from the personal to the national, as the third passes from the national to the world-wide.

> 'The devil taketh him into the holy city; and he set him on the pinnacle of the temple.'

> 'If thou be the Son of God, said he, cast thyself down and angel hands shall bear thee up. Dazzle

the people into faith; give them a sign, that they may believe' (Matt 4:5-6).

The essence of this temptation is that he should accommodate himself to the prejudices of the multitude, the traditions of the scribes, the vested interests of the priests. We seem to note in the Gospels a willingness on the part of the rulers to acknowledge Jesus as a prophet and teacher, provided that he should compromise on those points which most closely affected them. That he should, for example, do nothing to interfere with those monopolies which had made the house of Annas almost incredibly wealthy; that he should accept the unwritten law of the rabbis as of binding authority; that he should be willing to become a mere miracle-worker, in order that the people might be impressed by spectacular displays of supernatural power.

'Cast thyself down,' said the tempter. It may be, as some have affirmed, that the Jews in our Lord's time cherished the belief that the Messiah was to be revealed to Israel in a way like to that which the devil proposed. If our Lord had flung himself down, had been upborne by angel hands, and had stood by the great altar where the people were gathered for the morning sacrifice, it is possible that they would have acclaimed him the Anointed of God.

But what would such faith be worth? There would be in it no sorrow for sin, no longing for holiness, no endeavour after new obedience. If later, on the mountain-side, he had received from the multitude who 'craved for bread and nothing else' the crown and throne of David, what manner of royalty would this have been for him who came to save his people from their sins? Or, again, if he had submitted to the subtle machinations of the priestly party, had infused into the nation a militant patriotism, and had precipitated a revolt against the might and majesty of Rome, how would this beseem him who came to shed no blood but his own? 'Move along the plane of least resistance,' says the tempter; 'use the tools that lie to your hands; make the best of existing conditions; compromise.' Jesus answers: 'It is written, Thou shalt not tempt the Lord thy God.'

(c) The third and last temptation goes out to the uttermost parts of the earth. These had been promised to the Messiah by the Father from of old. Now Satan assumes the right of governance, saying, in full view of the wealth and dominion of earth: 'All these things will I give thee, if thou wilt fall down and worship me' (Matt 4:9). If we think that this proposal is too outrageous to awaken anything but repulsion in the mind of the Master, let us remember that he himself has stripped the glamour from this sin, revealing it to us in its native hideousness.

From the hill behind his home in Nazareth

our Lord would often look upon the ships of Tarshish, sailing out towards the Pillars of Hercules, or returning to Tyre and Sidon with precious consignments. He would watch the slow caravans coming from Mesopotamia, Sheba and Damascus, and at times he would trace the march of Roman legionaries along the great north road. Already, in his boyhood, he had come to know something of the kingdoms of this world and their glory.

And now, from this exceeding high mountain, he sees the flash of gold and the glitter of steel. He is made aware of exquisite harmonies and glorious artistic imaginings. He comes to know the craft of statesmanship, the advance of science, the range of philosophic thought. And Satan seems to say, 'By these thou shalt win the world.' The force of the insolent demand that Jesus should recognize the suzerainty of the prince of evil lies, it may be, in the presumption that sin belongs to the nature of man, and may be expelled, nay, must be, by natural means. If, in the upward process of development, we have passed from the lowest forms of non-moral savagery, we must still proceed, it has been said, along that upward path, shedding the vestiges of a lower creation, and evolving righteousness and truth by persistent tracking of high ideals. But attractive as this scheme appears to many, it possesses two fatal flaws: it asserts that sin is native to the soul, and it denies the virtue of the Cross of Christ.

On the mountains of Quarantania Jesus lifted up his eyes and saw the vision which Ezekiel had once beheld, which John the beloved was yet to see - 'the frame of a city towards the south'; a city whose walls are salvation, whose gates are praise. Those gates are open continually, day and night, for there is no night there. And through the uplifted portals there streams a multitude that no man can number, arrayed in white robes, with palms in their hands, singing the new song of redeeming love, and pressing over the golden ways to the throne of God and the Lamb. And Jesus, turning from the tempter with the stern word, 'Get thee behind me, Satan,' sets his face towards the hill of shame, still far away, but soon to be surmounted by a cross.

CHAPTER FOUR

ALL PRAYER

St Paul mentions 'all prayer' as one of the weapons in the armoury of God (Eph 6:18). Our Lord, it need hardly be said, engaged in all manner of prayer.

1

We may contemplate him first as sharing in social and public intercession.

(a) We think of him as uniting in worship with all the children of faith, as it is written: 'In the midst of the congregation will I sing praise unto thee' (Heb 2:12). At the opening of his ministry he proceeded, 'as his custom was' to the Nazareth synagogue. Sabbath after Sabbath, he associated himself in prayer and thanksgiving with all the men and women of good will who met there for worship.

Afterwards, in the temple and at the ritual feasts, he would certainly join in the services of the law. In his opening manhood, as the responsibilities of life were claiming his peculiar care, he reminded his parents of his duty as an Israelite: 'Wist ye not that I must be in my Father's house?' (Luke 2:49). In his inaugural mission to Jerusalem he described the temple as a house of prayer for all nations.

When, after his departure, his disciples were continually in the temple giving thanks to God, it is probable that they were to some extent influenced by their Master's example.

In one respect, as we have already said, his prayers would not be in unison with those of other worshippers - he knew no sin; he had no personal confession to present. Yet he was even then, in the eternal decree, bearing the guilt of men - Sin-bearer for the race. In his intercession he was already taking upon himself our trespass; as the Mediator he accepted responsibility for the sins of the whole world.

(b) It is evident also that our Lord was accustomed to unite with his disciples in a common supplication. They and he, for example, would join in the 'Thanksgiving for the breaking of bread' at the daily meal. On the mountain-side, according to his wont, he blessed the Giver of all good, as he took into his hands the meagre supplies that were to be increased to meet the needs of the many. At the Supper-table he, as Ruler of the Feast, 'gave thanks'. This act of worship may have been in addition to the form of words prescribed for use at the Passover. We may think of it as a fervent outpouring of spirit, as the Scottish paraphrase suggests:

And after thanks and glory given
To him that rules in earth and heaven,
That symbol of his flesh he broke,
And thus to all his followers spoke.

The prayer which closed the Paschal celebration was, as we know, one that rose immeasurably above the ritual of the festival. It is recorded, for our admonition and strengthening in love, in the seventeenth chapter of the Gospel according to St John. It is, if we may use the phrase, a high example of the 'family worship' with which our Lord and his disciples were wont to close the day.

(c) But this prayer was, in addition, a priestly act. Although he was not of the lineage of Aaron, our Lord was, upon earth, one chosen from among men in things pertaining to God. As in Ephraim he had taken the little children in his arms, laying his hands on them as he made intercession on their behalf, so, in the valley of the Kidron, he blesses with uplifted hands the Church which he is about to purchase with his blood:

'I pray for those whom thou hast given me... neither for these only do I pray, but for them also that believe on me through their word...that the world may believe that thou didst send me' (John 17).

This is the only sustained prayer of Christ which has been given to us. As one has truly said:

'We cannot thankfully enough wonder at and magnify the goodness of God, who has taken care that one of the prayers in which the Son of God poured out his heart to the Father should be so carefully communicated to us.' As we listen to those words of our Covenant-Surety, it is as if a door were opened in heaven, and we beheld the Lamb in the midst of the throne.

The last act of our Saviour's ministry was in the power of an unchangeable priesthood:

'He led them out until they were over against Bethany: and he lifted up his hands, and blessed them.'

As he blessed them, he was parted from them, and was carried up into heaven. That unfinished blessing rests upon his Church today. The Amen will be uttered only on his return in the glory of the Father, apart from sin, unto salvation.

2

Let us speak next of his solitary communings. Sometimes he went forth to pray 'a great while before day' (Mark 1:35), at other times he outwatched the stars (Matt 14:25), once at least he spent the entire night in supplication (Luke 6:12).

'Cold mountains and the midnight air
Witnessed the fervour of his prayer.'

He had much to say to the Father, much to hear.

Each of the Evangelists commemorates the prayer-life of Jesus, but it is St Luke who brings it before us in the fullest detail. The beloved physician may have learned something of the worth and power of prayer from St Paul, his great-hearted travelling companion, who poured his life out in intercession, 'night and day praying exceedingly' (1 Thess 3:10). Because of that high example St Luke would be the more able to appreciate this aspect of the Lord's service on our behalf.

In Luke 5:16 we have a general statement which throws a vivid light on the daily practice of the Master: 'And he withdrew himself in the deserts, and prayed.' It is not of one occasion, but of many, that the Evangelist speaks in this place. It was our Lord's habit to seek retirement for prayer; when he withdrew himself from men, he was accustomed to press far into the uninhabited country - he was *in the deserts*. In this sentence the emphatic word is the pronoun 'he'. The surprise of the onlookers lay in this, that One so mighty, so richly endowed with spiritual power, should find it necessary for himself to repair to the sources of strength, that there he might refresh his wearied spirit.

To us the wonder is still greater - that he, the Prince of Life, the Eternal Word, the Only-begotten of the Father, should prostrate himself in meekness before the throne of God, making entreaty for grace to help in every time of need. The only explanation to be given is that, in coming into manhood, he accepted life under those conditions to which our human nature has been subjected. He 'came forth' from God, he 'came down' among men, he 'became poor' for our sakes, he 'emptied himself' of the dignities and splendours of Deity.

Bordering on the Lake of Galilee there is a strip of uncultivated territory, termed 'the mountain,' a rough belt of untrimmed pasture-land, rising swiftly from the margin of the lake to the plateau above. Here our Lord often sought and found a sequestered spot, where he might hold uninterrupted communion with his Father.

The open air had a particular charm for Jesus. The intense simplicities of nature wrap the soul in silence, falling around one like the curtains of the sanctuary. In the glory of sunset, in the hush of a starlit evening, in the pallid pureness of the dawn, God seems to draw near: the clang of machinery no longer fills our ears; we hear his voice in the garden.

It is probable that our Lord, according to the Eastern mode (1 Sam 1:13) was wont to offer prayer audibly. This is, I think, implied in Luke 11:1:

'It came to pass, as he was praying in a certain place, that when he ceased, one of his disciples said unto him, Lord, teach us to pray.'

The disciples, having drawn near, heard a solemn sound as of one praying: they stood, hushed in reverence, until he rose and joined them.

But there was a still deeper need for solitude in the hour of prayer. Prayer is our entrance into the secret place, where our Father seeth (Matt 6:6).

Both by word and by example the Lord Jesus impressed upon his disciples the importance of solitude in prayer. At one time he enters the tiny store-chamber and shuts the door (Matt 6:6), at another he makes his way toward a solitary place (Mark 1:35); again, he ascends the hill-scarp (Mark 6:46) or the high mountain (Luke 9:28), and often he leaves the city behind him and finds an oratory in the Olive Garden (Luke 22:39).

We have reason to believe that he frequently united in prayer with his disciples, but we read that often at such times he would withdraw from them. He called his disciples apart to Caesarea Philippi, to inform them that his rejection by the rulers of Israel had been determined on, and that his death was at hand; in that place they seem to have spent a week in prayerful retreat, yet even there he separated himself from them: 'It came to pass as he was praying alone, the disciples were with him' (Luke 9:18) - alone, even then.

And as they proceeded on the last journey to the City of the Great King,

'They were in the way going up to Jerusalem, and Jesus was going before them; and they were amazed; and as they followed, they were afraid. And he took again the twelve, and began to tell them the things that were to happen unto him' (Mark 10:32).

Once more, on the night of his betrayal and arrest, after he had offered the High-Priestly prayer in the audience of his disciples, he withdrew from them. To the eight he said: 'Sit ye here, while I go yonder and pray' (Matt 26:36); then, leaving the favoured three, he went a little farther into the sombre wood (verse 39) and fell on his face and prayed.

It is difficult for many of the Lord's children to find privacy for prayer, and into such an experience he himself has entered. In the days of his youth he was one of a large family, crowded into a little cottage.

Amid the vicissitudes of his ministry he was in journeyings oft, lodging perhaps in the wayside khans.

He was frequently the guest of those whose opportunities of offering a place for retirement in prayer were severely restricted; at other times his hosts were careless of his needs.

But always he sought means for private prayer.

Instinctively, as well as in accordance with habit, we close our eyes when we pray. This attitude is the outward sign of inward recollection. We shut out from our view the world of sense, so that we may concentrate thought on that which is unseen and eternal. The intrusion of ordinary interests would confuse our mind, the presence of even our dearest friend would prevent the closing in upon us of the powers of the world to come. In abstraction from all that is created, we come to realise the essential things of the spirit.

In the silence God has much to say to us. He comes to search and try, to throw illumination into the dark places of our nature, to discover what of secret and undiscovered sin may be in us, to reveal to us his holiness, justice and love, and to bring us into a rejoicing harmony with his thrice-blessed will.

3

In the presence of others the Saviour seems often to have been immersed in the prayer of silence.

When the woman of Canaan besought him on behalf of her daughter, he answered her not a word (Matt 15:23). It has been suggested that, as her request would have carried him beyond his commission - 'I am not sent but to the lost sheep of the house of Israel' - he 'telegraphed home for instructions': hence his momentary silence.

When the man who was deaf and had an impediment in his speech was brought to Jesus, our Lord, looking up to heaven, sighed, and said, *'Ephphatha'*. The look was prayer, the sigh also, then followed the word of power. The word so spoken rang in Simon's memory: he felt that no translation could worthily render it. In relating this incident to his catechumens, even to those whose familiar speech was Greek, he felt himself impelled to give the word precisely as Jesus uttered it. Accordingly, it stands in the original Aramaic in the Gospel which John Mark wrote under the guidance of Simon Peter (Mark 7:34).

When, on his return from Peraea, the Lord came to Bethany, his purpose was not only to comfort the sorrowing sisters, but to raise their brother from the dead. For power to effect this he prayed. We learn only incidentally of this silent supplication - when the Lord drew near to the sepulchre, he lifted up his eyes to heaven and said: 'Father, I thank thee that thou heardest me' (John 11:41). May we not believe that, as soon as the appeal to mercy reached his ears, there was a swift uplifting of his heart to the Father and an answering gift of power? His unspoken prayer has been accepted; and now there is open acknowledgement before the people.

When the seventy evangelists returned to Jesus and told him of their spiritual successes, told him also of the antagonisms which they had encountered, 'He rejoiced in the Holy Spirit'; then broke forth in thanksgiving. In those words of praise he seems to refer to prayer offered for them during their absence, 'I beheld Satan as lightning fallen from heaven' (Luke 10: 17-24).

The Evangelists relate that on the morning of the second day of Passion Week our Lord, as he passed by, spoke to the barren fig tree, and immediately it withered away. Next morning the disciples drew his attention to the drooping leaves and Jesus, taking the fruitless tree as his text, read them a lesson on prayer, earnest and believing. We may judge that his words of doom to the pretentious but barren fig tree were uttered after a silent communication had been addressed to his Father.

No mention is made of prayer in Mark 10:32, but we are constrained to think of it: 'And they were in the way, going up to Jerusalem; and Jesus was going before them: and they were amazed; and they that followed were afraid.' Our Lord is advancing, to meet and break the power of hell. All his faculties are concentrated on the work which his Father has given him to do. His face is 'set like a flint', he quickens his steps, the disciples fall behind, shaken to consternation, stung with fear. Was there not in the mind of our Lord on that crowded pilgrim way a prelude to the Gethsemane agony?

We cannot but believe that an incessant stream of prayer flowed upward from the heart of the Man of Sorrows during the course of his ministry.

Again and again it breaks forth in arrow-flights of prayer and ejaculatory thanksgivings.

Indeed, we are certain that, in the nature of things, it must have been so. Our Lord is foreshown in the experiences of the saintly life commemorated in the Old Testament, as when it is said in the Psalter: 'I am prayer' (Psalm 109:4), and in the Prophets: 'He wakeneth morning by morning. He wakeneth mine ear to hear as they that are taught' (Isa 1:4).

In the Gospels this continual intercourse with the Father is plainly asserted in many passages:

> 'Verily, verily, I say unto you, The Son can do nothing of himself, but what he seeth the Father doing: for what things soever he doeth, these the Son doeth in like manner... I can of myself do nothing: as I hear, I judge... I do nothing of myself; but as the Father taught me, I speak these things... I speak the things which I have seen with my Father' (John 5:19, 30; 8:28,38).

So undeviating was this fellowship of spirit between the Father and the Son that we read in one passage of 'the Son of Man which is in heaven' (John 3:13). On earth he had nowhere to lay his head; his home was in heaven. More than once the Saviour speaks of himself as having, during his earthly sojourn, his dwelling in the Presence-chamber of God:

'If any man serve me, let him follow me; and where I am, there shall also my servant be.' 'I come again, and will receive you unto myself; that where I am, there ye may be also.' 'Father, that which thou hast given me, I will that, where I am, they also may be with me' (John 12:26; 14:3; 17:24).

CHAPTER FIVE

BEFORE THE CALLING OF THE TWELVE

'And it came to pass in those days, that he went out into the mountain to pray; and he continued all night in prayer to God. And when it was day, he called his disciples; and he chose from them twelve, who also he named apostles' (Luke 6:12,13).

It is stated only once that Jesus continued all night in prayer. He may have spent other nights in intercession, but there is no report of his having done so. Our Lord's spirit was maintained in calmness. His life was strenuous from the first, it deepened in intensity, but it was without strain. His days were filled with laborious service, and his physical frame demanded rest in sleep. One may, therefore, estimate the importance of this occasion in the view of our Master, when, in preparation for the calling of the Twelve, he spent the night in prayer.

From among his followers he is to select twelve, who during his days on earth shall be eye-witnesses and ministers of the Word, and after his resurrection the heralds of his return. He is to choose a company of men, who, by their testimony and doctrine, shall lay the foundations of the spiritual temple - men of open-air life, quick to observe and honest to report, who will not construe history in terms of a cherished theory; men of uprightness, who will adorn the doctrine that they preach, who in all good conduct will demean themselves after the pattern of their Lord; men who will be so firmly convinced of the truth which they profess as to be willing to die for the vindication of it, who will love their Master more than life, and will seek first the interest of his Kingdom.

The duties that were to be laid on the apostles were - to testify to the facts of the Saviour's ministry, beginning from the baptism of John until the day that he was received up; to create the apostolic tradition out of which the New Testament has grown; and to found on earth the Church which he has redeemed by his blood.

As we well know, almost all of those who were chosen were faithful men, whose hearts God had touched; they were unskilled in Jewish casuistry; they were not deeply versed in Scripture truth; in some degree, they were lacking in spiritual perception. But now they are about to enter the school of Christ, and there is no teacher like him. He spent a great, perhaps the greater, part of his brief ministry in training them in knowledge and godly fear. At the first they were probably like ourselves - ordinary people - but they became the foundation pillars of the New Jerusalem.

We may form some idea of the change which

passed over them, as they followed Jesus in the way and hearkened to his word, by the transformation which we are able to observe in the case of two of those selected ones - Peter and John. When we compare what is written of them in the Gospels with that which we may read between the lines in their Epistles, we find that in the early days of discipleship Simon Peter is sometimes rude, blundering, quarrelsome, whereas as he nears the goal he is courteous, lowly, of fair and gentle speech. The beloved disciple, too, was impetuous, narrow of outlook, and stinted in charity - a veritable son of thunder; but he became, after him who has no peer, the highest embodiment on earth of Christian love.

Those elements which Christ wrought to perfect nobleness were already present in the character of those disciples whom he was about to call to the apostolate. They were 'his own'; he had begun a good work in them; and his prescient eye saw whereto it would tend. In prayer on the mountain he asks that those aptitudes and endowments which he discerns in them shall be brought to perfectness by the Spirit of holiness. It was as if he foresaw the course of their lives, through temptation, persecution, and distress; he gauged their peril, he detected the snares set for their feet by the great adversary, and he prayed for them, that they might not be turned out of the way, but be faithful until the end.

Nor can we suppose that his intercession was arrested at the point where those faithful ones sealed their testimony in death. All down the ages their influence has gone, and wherever the fruit of their labour has been found, there the prayer of the Lord Jesus has preceded. This night of prayer must have besought and secured the welfare of the Church until, under the flaming skies and the rending heavens, the warrior service of the Bride shall cease.

'Judas Iscariot, who also betrayed him'; all the lists end with this sorrowful announcement. We naturally ask how it was that he should become one of the Twelve. Was not Jesus able to read the deep secrets of his character? Undoubtedly he was. St John tells us, 'Jesus knew from the beginning who they were that believed not, and who it was that should betray him' (John 6:44). Our Lord was not deceived.

We may credit the tradition that Judas was at first most earnest, that of all the disciples he was the most convincing preacher and the most powerful exorcist. He soon forced his way to the front rank in the apostolic company; he was appointed to an office of trust; he seems to have aspired to the highest place. Many, no doubt, regarded him as the most promising of the Master's followers; others would hesitate, judging that a flame so fierce and heady might as quickly expire. But Jesus knew; he needed not any should testify of man, for he knew what was in man. Why, then, did he receive the traitor into the number of the elect?

Does not our Lord still act in this way? Does he not often accept a man on his own profession, that he may challenge him to make that profession good? Was there not afforded through that calling an opportunity of salvation to this dark-natured man? Robert McCheyne tells us that our Lord, in his tender and wistful forbearance to his treacherous follower, endeavoured to the last to 'melt the betrayer'. We may be sure that such patient efforts to restore the wanderer had never been lacking: but all was in vain. Intimate fellowship with the Redeemer might have opened a way of hope to this unhappy man; but now the Lord himself is forced to lament: 'What could I have done more than I have already done?'

We may, however, see another reason for the inclusion of Judas among the Twelve. The primary duty of the apostles was to bear witness to Christ. They lived with him in the most perfect intimacy; in his relations with them there was no restraint. They saw more clearly than others his pure simplicity, the transparency of his perfect truth. They gazed on him with eyes of love, and said: 'He is holy, harmless, undefiled, separate from sinners.'

But that this interior testimony might be complete, it was necessary that it should be confirmed by one who did not love. After a time the interest which Judas may at first have found in Jesus gave place to a dull hatred, which deepened into a deadly malignity. But he, watching in the inner circle with keen eyes of malice, was able to see in his grievously wronged Master nothing but holiness and truth, until, with the heat of hell burning in his bones, Judas flung the base silver on the sanctuary floor, exclaiming: 'I have sinned in that I have betrayed innocent blood' (Matt 27:4).

All this would mingle in our Saviour's supplications in those dark hours upon that lonely hill.

CHAPTER SIX

AFTER THE FEEDING OF THE 5,000
(Matthew 14: 13-34)

The news of the death of the Baptist seems to have come to our Lord's ears shortly before the return of the Twelve from their first missionary journey. For the relief of his mind and theirs, and in order that he might hear more at leisure the report which the disciples had to give - 'whatsoever they had done and whatsoever they had taught' - he proposed that they should cross the lake, to reach some sequestered spot where they might be free from intrusion. So they 'went away in the boat to a desert place apart.'

The crowds, however, who were gathered in Capernaum, marked the boat's direction, and, running along the shore, 'outwent them'. When the little vessel drew to land, the beach was black with waiting forms - men, for the most part, though women and children were there also. It was the time of the Passover celebration, and all Israel was keeping holiday. As the day wore on to afternoon, and the multitudes still hung upon his lips, our Lord spread a table in the wilderness and fed the hungry with good things.

An undesirable result followed: a simultaneous movement ran through the crowd - this should be their King. They would compel him to receive at their hands the throne of his father David. Wages were meagre, taxes were weighty, food was dear: Jesus was one who could understand the lot of toiling men: he was able to sympathize with them in their arduous course; moreover, he was clothed with divine power. If only he were to consent to rule over them, life would become restful and glad, for he would remove the heavy burden and undo the yoke.

Jesus had once before been asked to receive a kingdom. That was offered by the tempter, and he had refused it, although crown and sceptre were his by covenant right. It was within his commission to preach glad tidings to the poor, to heal the broken-hearted, to proclaim release to the captives, and recovering of sight to the blind, to set at liberty them that were bound, to announce the year of the Lord's release (Luke 4:16-21).

But the Cross stood full in view, and he refused to turn aside. The time of which the Psalmist said, 'He shall judge the poor of the people, he shall save the children of the needy, and shall break in pieces the oppressor,' would come in its appointed season, but his hour was not yet. Jesus therefore 'constrained the disciples to enter into the boat, and to go before him unto the other side, till he should send the multitudes away.'

Evidently the multitudes were unwilling to

depart, and our Lord had to put an unwonted pressure upon them; at last they yielded to his insistence, and reluctantly withdrew to their homes. From a worldly point of view this action of the Lord appeared to be disastrous. It quenched the enthusiasm of the crowd, so that, 'from that time many of his disciples went back, and walked no more with him.'

St Mark gives us the explanation: 'They understood not concerning the loaves, but their heart was hardened' (Mark 6:52). It was a Passover festival over which the Lord had presided on the mountain-side, a feast upon the sacrifice. The breaking of the bread was anticipatory of his decease. As he afterward reminded them, they had been sacramentally eating his flesh and drinking his blood (John 6:51-58). The miracle of the loaves was an acted parable, designed to teach that every good gift received from Christ was offered by a hand that was pierced, was conveyed in the power of a life laid down.

When our Lord had sent the multitudes away, he went up into the mountain to pray. Meanwhile the disciples were rowing out into the storm at his word. As they bent over the oars, one at least marvelled at the Lord's absence: 'It was now dark, and Jesus had not yet come to them' (John 6:17). He saw them, however, from his lofty station, in the fitful gleams of the moonlight, as the cloud-rack drifted past; he observed that they were 'distressed in rowing'; at the critical juncture he came to them, walking upon the sea.

We may conjecture that our Lord's prayer was, on this occasion as so often, a renewed acceptance of his atoning death. As formerly, in the Wilderness of Judaea, as later, in the Garden of Gethsemane, he confronts the Cross. He embraces it, saying in the great words of a prophetic scripture:

'Lo, I am come: in the roll of the book it is prescribed to me: I delight to do thy will, O my God; yea, thy law is within my heart' (Psalm 40: 7-8).

And the Father seals him for sacrifice - the Lamb of God, stooping down, lifting up, bearing, and carrying away the sin of the world. It would be an irreverence to try to conceive the manner in which his mind would deal with the situation presented to him. We dare not speculate upon those aspects of his propitiatory sufferings which may have passed before his view in that lonely vigil.

But we know that his prayer was heard, and that he emerged from the conflict more than conqueror. In lofty grandeur he passed out into the storm, exulting in spirit as he trod the foaming waves, their white crests firm as marble pillars under his feet. Probably some effulgence of the glory of God which had clothed him in that hour of self-surrender still hung about him as he drew near; for the disciples, imagining that they beheld a spirit, cried out in their alarm as he approached the little boat tossing in the waste of waters.

This incident, conveying to us, as it does, intimations of the mind of Christ, is charged with an ampler meaning than that which the text directly affords. We may read into it a revelation of the mystery of the Saviour's intercession. He has ascended the hill of God, and now advocates our cause before his Father. His Church is on the storm-vexed sea, under command to gain the farther shore: his disciples labour without intermission, but make no headway, for the winds are contrary. They are in the midst of the lake, the boat is filling, and is ready to sink. It is now dark, and Jesus has not yet come to them. But he sees and understands; every motion of the quivering vessel, every curl of the threatening waves, is clear to his view.

His followers are preserved in faithfulness, they are held in safety, by his prayers. At length - it is now the fourth watch of the night - the morning breaks over the unquiet deep: he comes. Vested in uncreated light, he seeks his own, swiftly hasting on his way through the rage of the tempest. The exhausted rowers receive him gladly into the boat, and immediately they are at the haven whither they would be. The storm is past, the toil is over, the night is at an end: the Lord has come.

CHAPTER SEVEN

ON THE MOUNT OF VISION

1

Our Lord had left the territories ruled over by Herod Antipas, and had crossed into the tetrarchate of Philip; partly, on account of the threatening attitude of the Herodians, but chiefly, we may suppose, that he might in seclusion have the opportunity of instructing his disciples as to the certainty and manner of his approaching death. The Cross has come in sight; and it is needful that he should tell them plainly that 'the Son of Man must be crucified'. A week was spent in the neighbourhood of Caesarea, as in retreat - in prayer and conference.

On what was probably the evening of the seventh day Jesus, along with three of his disciples - those who presumably were the most apt to understand the lessons which the Transfiguration was fitted to teach - began to ascend one of the spurs of 'that goodly mountain' Hermon, which towers above the plain and dominates the landscape. It lay across the frontier of the Holy Land, for this revelation was not to be given to Israel only, but to the world.

We can still trace the path they took; first,

among the vineyards; afterwards through the corn-lands, and up among the olive-gardens to the groves of cypress and acacia. Beyond, the slopes were clothed with dense undergrowth, emitting fragrance from aromatic plants; higher still the black rock looked through the thinning vegetation, while the snow-crowned summit gleamed overhead. But this knot of wayfaring men was not making for the crest of the mountain; they sought some retired place of prayer, where they might be 'apart, by themselves' (Luke 9:28-36).

They came to this mountain oratory to pray, to pray about death, the death of the Prince of Life. Our Lord went up to embrace his Cross, and the disciples asked that they might enter into the fellowship of his sufferings. The prayers of the Chosen Three were soon over. They wrapped their heads in their mantles, and went to sleep. But the Lord prayed on. He was girding himself for his death-conflict. He repeated, as the fringe of the desolating storm of judgment crept towards him, the words which he had spoken from the Bosom of God in the eternal ages: 'Lo, I come... I delight to do thy will, O my God.' In the volume of the Book, the roll of the divine decrees, written before the foundation of the world, it had been prescribed to him. And as he prayed, he was transfigured.

The sense of something strange occurrent,

which so often startles a sleeper out of slumber, unsealed the heavy eyes of the disciples. For a moment they struggled with the torpor that had overpowered them, then 'when they were awake, they saw.'

They saw Jesus, transfigured before them. His form was as the light, his countenance was as the sun when it shineth in its strength. His glance was like lightning, and his homely, travel-stained garments became white and glistening, as the fine linen of the priestly vestments, or as moonlight upon snow.

This was not such a glory as fell on the upturned face of Moses, when in the cleft of Sinai he gazed upon God; nor was it like the angel brightness that shone as an aureole on Stephen's brow. These were from without; they were the reflection of the Uncreated Glory. But the transfiguration of the Saviour was from within; the indwelling Deity was irradiating the garment of flesh, which till now had veiled its splendour. It was the first open manifestation of the Christ as he truly is and eternally shall be. The disciple of love says:

'We beheld his glory, glory as of the only begotten from the Father, full of grace and truth' (John 1:14).

And Simon Peter adds: 'We were eye-witnesses of his majesty' (1 Pet 2:16). St Paul, who was not himself an eye-witness, gives testimony to the recollection of the early Church, when he alludes to 'the illumination of the knowledge of the glory of God in the face of Jesus Christ' (2 Cor 4:6).

Moses and Elijah were seen standing beside the Lord. 'The power to recognise them was granted with the power to see them.' Moses the lawgiver, and Elijah the reformer of Israel and first of the greater prophets, together with the Messiah, represent the full content of the divine revelation.

Simon arranges these in one series: Christ is first of the three, it is true, but in the same rank: in Simon's view we have 'Christ and other masters.' 'Master,' said he, 'it is a good thing that we are here; allow us to erect three booths of branches - one for thee, and one for Moses, and one for Elijah.' Truly, he was bewildered, and knew not what to say. Love speaks out of the confusion: 'One for thee, and one for Moses, and one for Elijah.'

What of themselves? Either they do not think of themselves at all, and that is love's way; or, and this also is the manner of love, it did not occur to them to think of any other abiding-place than that which should receive their Lord. They would not acknowledge any other home, nor could they endure the thought of being separated from him. Where he is, there we shall be also - this was the ineradicable conviction of their minds. A dying saint was asked about his hopes for heaven. 'Where else can I go?' he replied. Where, indeed, can the true lover of Jesus be but with his Lord? For:

'This I do find:
We two are so joined,
He'll not be in glory,
And leave me behind.'

Yet when Simon classed the Lord with Moses and Elijah, even though he placed our Saviour first in the series, God interposed. The Cloud of the Glory descended; and when it passed, Moses and Elijah were no longer visible upon the Mount: the disciples 'saw no man save Jesus only.' And a voice from the Cloud, a voice like the sound of many waters, the peal of a trumpet, or the noise of mighty thunderings - 'such a voice,' exclaims Simon, as he recalls it - a voice of divine authority, proclaimed: 'This is my beloved Son; hear him.'

Christ outranks all classification; he outsoars all grandeur: he has a name that is above every name. As one of the Scots worthies was wont to repeat: 'There is none like Christ; there is none but Christ.' He is peerless and alone; there is no other with him. Simon had been struggling towards this conception during the three years of his discipleship, but he had not yet attained to it. He had often differed in judgment from his

Lord; he had at times treated him with undue familiarity, even with disrespect. Yet at intervals it broke in upon his mind that Jesus of Nazareth was greater than he seemed. His stricken cry: 'Depart from me, for I am a sinful man, O Lord' (Luke 5:8), and his tardy but deliberate decision: 'Lord, to whom shall we go? Thou hast the words of eternal life' (John 6:6-8), prove this. Now he begins to learn that, in the most absolute sense, the Prophet of Galilee is God's only and well-beloved Son.

This truth was too great, too illustrious, to be received in a moment. It evidenced itself insensibly like the dawn. The day began to lighten, a shaft of cold light stirred the eastern sky, pale gleams of saffron pierced the cloud-rack, the day-star trembled on the horizon; then swiftly came the rush of morning glory, and now - the sun is uprisen. In later years Simon found no words in which he might worthily celebrate the praises of his Lord. This Jesus the Nazarene had received a name all names excelling; he had filled heaven with his glory and earth with his power; from his mediatorial throne he was ruling the ages and marshalling the circling years.

2

In their earthly life Moses and Elijah had seen Christ's day afar off. Moses stood by the altar reared under the crags of Sinai, and when he had sprinkled the people with the blood of sacrifice, he announced: 'Behold, the blood of the covenant, which the Lord hath made with you concerning all these words' (Exod 24:8). Elijah repaired the desecrated altar of Jehovah on Carmel, and invoked that Sacred Name, until the fire of God fell and consumed the offering (1 Kings 18:16-45). But both these fathers of the faith understood clearly that the blood of bulls and of goats could not take away sin; therefore, they looked forward to one whose coming had been foretold - a Prince and a Saviour.

Moses died at the mouth of the Lord, and Elijah was borne up to heaven in a whirlwind. In the Upper Sanctuary they had had for centuries communion with him who is the Firstborn of all creation, the express Image of Jehovah's Person. After protracted companionship, with the pre-incarnate but already manifested Word, it has been permitted to them to return to earth, to hold converse with the Word made flesh.

When the Wilderness Journeyings were drawing to a close, Moses preferred one last request: 'Let me go over, I pray thee, and see the good land that is beyond Jordan, that goodly mountain, and Lebanon' (Deut 3:25). His petition was not granted then: on the heights of Abarim he surveyed with undimmed eyes the Promised Land; then, God kissed him, and he slept (Deut 34:1-6). Now, however, after fourteen centuries, his prayer is granted; he actually stands upon the goodly mountain of his desire, and views the whole land of Immanuel in an ampler field of vision than that vouchsafed from Pisgah.

In the reaction which followed the triumphant vindication of Jehovah's sovereignty, Elijah fled to the desert of the fiery law. He vainly tried to find shelter under the spare branches and narrow leaves of a juniper bush, and prayed in stark despondency that he might die: 'It is enough; now, O Lord, take away my life; for I am not better than my fathers' (1 Kings 19:1-5). One has quaintly suggested that, as the prophet of fire rode royally into heaven, he looked down upon the desert shrub where, in the deep gloom of his spirit, he had called upon death.

To Moses and Elijah, therefore, death was not a novel experience, although it had, in the case of each, been swallowed up in victory.

An obscure phrase in the Epistle of Jude (verse 9) may be thought to imply that the body of Moses was raised 'out of due time' that he might take part in this earthly ministry of consolation rendered to the Saviour. On the other hand, the body of Elijah's humiliation was 'changed' as he went up into the glory of God. And as the transfiguration of our Lord is confessedly a symbol and pledge of his return and of our gathering together unto him, Moses and Elijah may remind us of those who shall welcome the

Redeemer as he comes to earth in his kingdom and power:

> *'The dead in Christ* shall rise first; then *we that are alive and remain* shall be caught up together with them in the clouds, to meet the Lord in the air: and so shall we ever be with the Lord' (1 Thess 4:16-17).

Moses and Elijah 'appeared in glory and spake of his decease which he was about to accomplish at Jerusalem.' The impression left on one's mind by the condensed report of this august interview is, that our Lord was the speaker, and that Moses and Elijah waited on his words for instruction. He explains to them matters relating to the mystery of atonement in a manner such as it had not been possible for them hitherto to understand.

The word translated 'decease' is literally 'exodus'; 'He spake of the exodus which he was about to accomplish at Jerusalem.'

The going forth of the Tribes from Egypt was not a defeat but a triumph. It had its origin in redemption - in the paschal sacrifice. As soon as the blood was sprinkled before the threshold of the slave-huts in Goshen, the Hebrew serfs received from God their manumission. With loins girt and with staff in hand they gathered to the Passover Feast. On that night, much to be remembered, they left the house of bondage. In the power of the blood of sprinkling they were made the freemen of the Lord Almighty.

Moses and the tribes of Israel stood by the shore of the sea, sheeted with storm-drift under the fury of a 'strong east wind'. As the lawgiver stretched his rod over the tumult, the waters parted, and the ransomed of the Lord went through the flood on foot. On the following day, as the sun poured its level rays across the now placid lake, gleaming like crystal dipped in flame, the happy people, radiant with thanksgiving, poured forth the song of Moses, the servant of God, and the song of the Lamb:

'Sing unto the Lord, for he hath triumphed gloriously: the horse and his rider hath he thrown into the sea. The Lord is my strength and song, and he is become my salvation; This is my God, and I will praise him; my father's God and I will exalt him' (Exod 15: 1-2).

Such were the sacred recollections in which the Saviour enshrined the Gospel of redeeming love, setting it forth in ancient phrase as by a parable.

In the power of his own blood he would go forth, the first-begotten from among the dead, the leader of the ransomed army, trampling upon tempestuous seas, and making his footsteps a way to walk in. He has entered into covenant, to deliver from servitude to sin and introduce to a life of holiness a multitude that no man can number, redeemed out of every nation and kindred and people and tongue. This exodus he 'was about to accomplish at Jerusalem.'

3

In taking the disciples with him up into the mountain he may have been impelled by a feeling akin to that which led him to say at the enclosure of Gethsemane's garden: 'Tarry ye here, and watch with me.' Our Lord was brave beyond all telling, but he was not stoically wrapped up in the pride of endurance. He craved the sympathetic fellowship of those whom he loved, and it belonged to his self-emptying here on earth that so few were able to understand his aims, and they only in the most restricted measure.

A gifted writer has told of a brilliant function: people of high degree were present; the whole scene was redolent of satisfaction and enjoyment. On the wall above the gay throng there hung, among other paintings, one of the Saviour, thorn-crowned and blood-bedewed, treading the wine-vat. No one but the writer seemed to notice the picture, but as she observed it, she remembered the words: 'I have trodden the wine-press *alone.*'

'Alone, O Christ, yea, evermore alone,
In that strange anguish, even when close to thee
Thy people press with tears.'

But here, as later in Gethsemane, the attendant disciples were unable to enter into the mind of their Lord. Thus it is, too often, alas, with us: we fail to realise the sorrow of his dying, his hunger for the salvation of men, the joy of his finished work.

But this consideration just touches the fringe of our subject.

From the slopes of Hermon, as the morning was about to break, our Saviour might review the scenes of his ministry. Far off, the ridge above Nazareth rose into sight; nearer, the waters of the Lake of Galilee flashed in the light of stars; here and there a cluster of dwellings, or a white edge of winding road, indicated the scenes of his mighty works. Samaria, Peraea, Judaea, oft trodden by his patient feet, lay stretched before him as in a map. In the distance, out of sight, Jerusalem sat enthroned upon her everlasting hills.

One can imagine the strain of our Saviour's thoughts as his eye rested on those familiar places - how he would enfold each town and village separately in his prayer of intercession, until his emotion may have burst forth in cries like these: 'Alas for thee, Chorazin, Bethsaida, Capernaum. Ye would not come unto me, that ye might have life. O Jerusalem, Jerusalem, how often would I have gathered thee.' All his ministry, now so near its close, is summarised in that night of prayer upon the Holy Hill.

And as he prayed he was transfigured. Perhaps it was not on this occasion only that such a transformation passed upon him.

After a night of prayer on the mountain-edge, where he had fed the thousands with the scanty store of a lad's wallet, he had walked, in singular elevation of spirit, across the storm-vexed lake; and when the disciples saw him, they cried out for fear. In that prolonged season of prayer Jesus had surrendered himself anew to the call of the Cross, and had therefore been crowned with glory and honour.

Again, at the gate of the Olive Garden, where he confronted the soldiers sent to arrest him, there seems to have been a majesty in his bearing that was not of earth, so that even the legionaries of Rome, seasoned and tested men, were flung backward on the grass as by the blow of an unseen hand. (John 18:6.)

Was it not the lingering glory of the acceptance of his passion that smote with terror the disciples in the one case, and in the other the soldiers?

It was as he prayed that his countenance was changed. At various times in our Lord's progress to the Cross the awful meaning of the agony that was before him fell upon his spirit with ever-increasing force. On each occasion there was a prelibation of the cup which his Father had given him to drink. The decision made in eternity had been ratified on earth again and again, each time with a more adequate comprehension of what it meant to be guilt-bearer for the world. And each renewal of his covenant engagement with the Father on our behalf had to be striven for through travail and dismay. In this transfiguration glory there must have been a mingling of emotion - love and pity, heroism and endurance, joy and peace. All the blended hues of heaven's light shone on the countenance that was lifted up to heaven in prayer on the mountain-side.

If we ask further what the transfiguration may have meant to Christ, we may observe these points: his righteousness was approved, his probation was brought to a close, his sacrifice was sealed, his reward was assured.

(a) *The righteousness of Christ was approved.* The Father regards the stainless life of Jesus and is satisfied: 'This is my beloved Son, in whom I am well pleased.' There was no blemish in his radiant character, no flaw in his perfect obedience. The years of childhood, of labour, and of ministry pass in review before God, and there is no fault in them. Had it been otherwise, the Son of Man could not have been our Saviour. The redemption of the soul is precious, and man must let that alone for ever: neither can he by any means redeem his brother, or give to God a ransom for him. But this man has never sinned; he is solitary and supreme. And on the ground of his stainless purity his sacrifice is accepted.

(b) *The probation of the Lord Jesus was complete*. It seems to be taught both in the Old Testament and in the New that man, if he had continued in innocence, would have been taken up into a spiritual existence, as those shall be who are alive and remain at the Coming of Christ. Our first parents, had they resisted temptation, would have been raised to a deathless state. But they sinned and fell, and death came by sin. Our Lord entered into the defeat and tragedy of our race.

> 'O loving wisdom of our God!
> When all was sin and shame,
> A second Adam to the fight
> And to the rescue came.'

And now, on the testimony of the Father, the probation of the Messiah is finished. When he had brought in an everlasting righteousness he went up into a high mountain and was transfigured. He received an abundant entrance into that state of spiritual being which they possess who stand in the Living Presence and gaze upon God. Heaven comes down to receive to itself this Heavenly One. The glorified saints of the ancient covenant are representatives of that great cloud of witnesses who surround the throne. The Shekinah-cloud rests on the hill; the Father utters his voice, as from the mercy-seat; Jesus of Nazareth, by right of his holy obedience, has entered into heaven. He has restored that which he had not taken away, he has magnified the law and made it honourable.

But he will not accept the glory due to him. The distressed and demon-ridden world is under his feet. He will not enter heaven alone. He came to condemn sin, not merely by winning an unbroken triumph over it, but rather by accepting the doom incurred by sinful men and by tasting death in their stead. He drew back from the opening heavens, descending the mountain, that he might climb the cross. 'He loved me, and gave himself for me.'

(c) *On the Mountain, the Lamb of God was sealed for sacrifice.* 'This is my beloved Son, in whom I am well pleased' - thus spake the Voice from the Cloud, or, as St Peter describes it, 'the Voice out of Heaven.' Our Lord was not merely an innocent victim, a spotless offering from the fields of earth: he was Jehovah's fellow. The word here rendered 'beloved' has a very significant meaning in Greek. It indicates the love that is lavished upon an only child; thus it bears the meaning here of 'sole-begotten', and reminds us of the Old Testament word: 'Take now thy son, thine only son Isaac, whom thou lovest' (Gen 22:2). It is as if the Father were recalling the scene on Moriah, two thousand years before, when Abraham, the friend of God, saw Christ's day and was glad.

(d) Once more, our Lord looked out through the travail of his soul, and knew *that his reward was assured*. Moses and Elijah stood before him as the earnest of his purchased possession. Behind them was a great company of the saints of the house of Israel clothed in white robes, lifting on high the palms of unending peace.

CHAPTER EIGHT

BLESSING THE CHILDREN

After the raising of Lazarus the death-warrant of
Christ was signed by the chief priests and the
Pharisees (John 11: 45-53). His hour was not yet
come; accordingly, he retired to Ephraim, a
mountain village on the edge of the desert, over-
looking the Jordan valley and the Dead Sea.
Here he seems to have passed several weeks, but
the history of those weeks is one of the unwritten
chapters of the Gospel (cf.: John 20:30; 21:25):
no incident relating to it has been preserved by
any of the Evangelists. We feel the sacredness of
the silence. Our Lord was girding himself for his
approaching warfare and suffering: he was dwelling in the secret of the Divine Presence, holding
intimate communion with the Father concerning the decease which he was shortly to
accomplish at Jerusalem.

Those days of retirement had apparently
drawn to an end, and our Lord was about to
descend into the pilgrim way, that he might
proceed with the Galilean company towards Jerusalem, when the parents of some young children
brought them to Jesus, that he might 'touch
them', as Mark and Luke have it, or, as we find it

in the First Gospel, 'that he should put his hands on them, and pray' (19: 13-15).

We speak of the 'mothers of Salem' but the word used here for those who brought their children to the Saviour is in the masculine; fathers as well as mothers crave for their little ones the benediction of the priestly hands of Christ. Among the Jews the father took an important share in the religious education of youth (cf.: Deut 6:6-9, 20-25 etc.). It was even customary for the parents of a little child to invite an illustrious rabbi, who might be passing near, to lay his hands on the young head in the name of Jehovah. The Aaronic blessing (Num 6:22-27) would probably be repeated, often, no doubt, with tenderness and deep feeling, for there must have been some of the Jewish doctors of whom it might have been said, as was reported of Henry Venn, that he never saw a young face without yearning to impart a spiritual gift.

But the disciples forbade them. It does not appear that those who surrounded the Master wished to censure an act which may have seemed to savour of superstition; for they would remember her who said: 'If I may but touch the hem of his garment, I shall be made whole.' Perhaps they wished to spare their Lord an intrusion which might not be welcomed; but they ought to have known that this was refreshment to him, not labour. It has been suggested that the precise form of the expression in Luke 18:16 - *Jesus called them unto him* - implies that 'it was a pleasure and a relief to him to have children near him.' It is often so; little children may be a fortress for troubled men: 'Out of the mouths of babes and sucklings hast thou ordained strength... that thou mightest still the enemy and the avenger' (Psalm 8:2).

Probably, however, the interference of the disciples was due to their spiritual dullness; they failed to realise the value of a child's soul. How greatly our Lord did prize this inestimable jewel is evident in the unwonted heat of his spirit, when he observed what they were about to do: he was 'moved with indignation' (Mark 10:14). This expression is nowhere else used with reference to our Lord. The only time of which it is said that his righteous anger overflowed its accustomed barriers was when his followers endeavoured to hold back the little ones who were pressing towards him.

This, I think, is what the narrative implies. May we not suppose that, during those quiet days spent in this highland village, the little ones had learned to trust the loving heart of the Saviour? And that now, as he is about to depart, they cluster round him, to offer a farewell greeting? Of their own act and deed they are coming to him, as to one whom they confide in and dearly love.

St Matthew tells us that some, at least, of the parents who brought their children to Jesus desired him to lay his hands upon them, *and pray*.

As is his wont, the Saviour does even more than they ask: he takes them up into his arms, clasps them to his heart, and blesses them fervently. The word translated 'blessed' conveys the idea of deep and tender feeling. It is often employed to denote a farewell salutation. Our Lord is going to Jerusalem, to die for these little ones; he folds them in his arms, presses them to his heart, and breathes upon them a blessing which ascends to God as prayer.

Sometimes, as we look upon the face of a little child, we are moved with compassion, as we reflect on the course of life that shall open before this young 'pilgrim of eternity'.

'O little feet! that such long years
Must wander on through hopes and fears
Must ache and bleed beneath your load;
I, nearer to the wayside inn,
Where toil shall cease and rest begin,
Am weary thinking of your load.'

Perhaps our Saviour, pausing in the village street to bless and intercede, saw, with more than a prophet's vision, the long uphillward path, sharp with stones and overgrown with mantling thorns, on which those baby feet would tread. And into his prayer would come the immeasurable tenderness of the love of God.

Those who brought their little ones to Jesus besought him that he would pray for them. Such a request could not be denied. May we not then believe that this one of our Lord's prayers would be fully answered? There is a tradition - though one without authority - that one of those little ones whom Jesus blessed was Ignatius of Antioch, apostle and martyr. May we not believe that all those children are now gathered around the Lamb who is the Shepherd of the ransomed flock?

'I wonder if ever the children
Who were blessed by the Master of old
Forgot he had made them his treasures,
The dear little lambs of his fold.

My heart cannot cherish the fancy
That ever those children went wrong,
And were lost from the peace and the shelter,
Shut out from the feast and the song.

To the day of grey hairs they remembered,
I think, how the hands that were riven
Were laid on their heads when Christ uttered,
'Of such is the kingdom of heaven'.'

Still godly parents are bringing their children to Jesus, and still the loving Saviour takes them up in his arms, lays his hands on them, and prays. Shall his prayer not be answered?

CHAPTER NINE

IN THE SCHOOL OF CHRIST

Our Lord gave his disciples many instructions regarding prayer; with the help of these we may discern some features which marked his own prayer-life.

1

Most impressive of all is his insistence on the closed door, which shuts in the solitary worshipper and shuts out the clamorous world. Of this we have spoken. Emphasis is also laid on the absence of ostentation in our religious exercises. Those who love to stand and pray in the synagogues and in the corners of the streets, that they may be seen of men, have in such recognition their sole reward. If one should resolve to fast in his supplications, let him anoint his head and wash his face, so as not to advertise his religious fervour. (Matt 6:5-18.)

Our Lord goes on to say that prayer should be simple, direct, and in ordinary cases, brief. Our Father knows what things we have need of; we do not have to persuade him to listen to us by our much speaking (Matt 6:5-8). This, I take it, is for the common strain of life. God is not far from any one of us; whenever we seek him, he waits to be gracious. In general, therefore, we do not need to persist in vociferous entreaty, 'battering the gates of heaven with storms of prayer.' A very beautiful verse (Mark 11:24) gives us knowledge of a better way: 'All things whatsoever ye pray and ask for, believe that ye have received them, and ye shall have them' (Mark 11:24). As soon as the prayer of faith ascends to God, the springs of power are touched, and remedial processes begin to work. We cast our burden on the Lord, and we learn that even before we called he had taken thought for us.

It appears therefore, that calm, brief, and trustful supplications are appropriate to the common things of life and to the daily task. But when we pass out into wider regions of the spirit, prayer assumes new forms.

When the disciples asked their Master why they had failed to expel the demon from the afflicted lad at the foot of the Mount of Transfiguration, our Lord replied: 'This kind can come forth by nothing save by prayer' (Mark 9:28-29). The familiar words, 'and fasting' are omitted by the Revisers. But even in the abbreviated sentence there is a hint of the stern urgency of the prayer that prevails. If it is unnecessary to storm heaven, it may yet be needful to break in pieces the gates of hell. When we are summoned to contend with powers of darkness in heavenly places, we must 'prevail to overcome'. There is an earnestness which bathes itself in passion, uttering itself even with strong crying and tears. It labours and wrestles, and strengthens itself to endure through an agony of supplication. Such was the prayer that broke the silence of the Olive Garden on the night that ushered in the death of the Redeemer. Darkness as of dereliction veiled the soul of the Sufferer; sweat as of blood bedewed his face and stained the trampled grass; but he came forth more than conqueror.

In two parables the Saviour teaches us that persistence such as will take no denial, but will press on even to 'shamelessness', is necessary when we intercede for the life of another; whether it be the individual worker praying that the bread of God might be ministered to him for the sake of his friend who is out of the way (Luke 11:6), or the widowed Church pleading for her children who have been fraudulently deprived of their birthright (Luke 18:7,8).

The formula in such cases is 'ask... seek... knock.'

We read that on one occasion our Lord 'in the morning, a great while before day, rose up and went out, and departed unto a desert place, and there prayed' (Mark 1:35). This was probably his daily usage. After a day prolonged until evening in teaching, healing, comforting, he rose early in the morning, that in undisturbed privacy he might hold communion with his Father. On this occasion he remained in his chosen solitude so long that 'Simon and they that were with him followed after him.' At the foot of 'the mountain' the people, curious and eager, were pressing round our Lord's dwelling.

When the disciples reached the mountain oratory Jesus was still in prayer. They listened, hushed to reverent feeling. When he had ceased, they say: 'Lord, teach us to pray, even as John also taught his disciples' (Luke 11:1). The Baptist had instructed his followers to repeat specified forms of address to God; Jesus had not done so. Now, at the request of Peter and his companions, he gives them the type and substance of all liturgies - the ordered series of petitions which we name 'The Lord's Prayer'.

The Saviour introduces this form of words with the injunction: 'When ye pray, say, Our Father.' God is the Father of those who seek him with a true and humble heart, and all are brethren in the family of God. In those two words *Our Father* we possess the key which unlocks the mystery of prayer. He knows what things we have need of before we ask him; it is his good pleasure to confer upon us every perfect gift. As the Creator, who built the framework of the heavens and instituted the order of nature, he is able to do exceeding abundantly above all that we ask or think, and he accepts responsibility for the maintenance and well-being of his children.

The construction of this prayer is extremely simple. Three great requests on behalf of the kingdom of God, three modest petitions for ourselves, are all that the Lord encourages us to present to the Father in heaven. For ourselves, daily bread, pardon continually renewed, grace to help in time of need - that is all. But for the kingdom these: 'Hallowed be thy name, thy kingdom come, thy will be done, as in heaven, so in earth.'

The triumphant conclusion, so familiar to our lips, is not in the earliest manuscripts. It comes to us rather as the voice of worshippers than as the saying of the Master. It is the invocation by the Church of the holy name of Jesus: 'For thine is the kingdom, and the power, and the glory, for ever.'

We may pass from the consideration of this form of prayer, for, though we call it by our Lord's name, it was spoken to his disciples.

The Master goes on to give an illustration of another mode of supplication. A liturgy must be supplemented by free request. No ritual form can full express the agony of Spirit-taught intercession which strives to communicate itself in groanings that cannot be uttered.

Our Lord then spoke a parable that breathes a quiet humour. (Luke 11:5-8.) A wayfarer forsakes the bridle-path which should lead him to his destination: he takes the wrong turning, and presently finds himself in an unfamiliar byway. He wanders on until the night begins to fall. Soon darkness arrests the steps of the belated traveller, who is now 'out of his way' (v 6, marg.). As he stumbles on, a gleam of light shines before him. Presently he comes to a tiny hamlet that is wrapped in slumber. Only one light burns; all others are quenched. The traveller asks admission into the house where the host still watches.

At once he is made welcome; whatever of hospitality this bare home can furnish is at his disposal; but there is no bread. The bread for the day has been consumed, the bread for tomorrow has not been baked. The master of the house cannot endure the thought that his guest should go fasting to bed. He hastily reviews the possibilities; he thinks of one neighbour on whose good will he may count. He goes to this one's house, arouses him, and *asks* for the loan of three cakes of bread. To his surprise, perhaps, he is refused: 'Trouble me not; the door is now shut, and my children are with me in bed; I cannot rise and give thee.' The answer is churlish, and its crude selfishness stirs the applicant.

He has been asking hitherto, now he begins to *seek*. He implores his friend in the name of common humanity to give this man, already faint with hunger, something to eat; he reminds him of the obligations of hospitality, and bids him reflect upon the disgrace which would attach to the village were it once known that bread to stay one's hunger had been denied. But the unkindly neighbour remains obdurate: he will not risk the sleepless hours that may fall upon the household if once the sleep of the children should be rudely broken.

The applicant has been *asking* and *seeking*, now he begins to *knock*. He is prepared, he says, to beat the door in; then, infallibly, the children will be roused. At this the neighbour takes swift alarm; he implores his friend to desist; he rises quietly, hurries to the door, and more than satisfies the needs of the troubler of his home.

This churlish neighbour - such is the boldness of some of our Lord's parables - represents God. The point, however, is not that our Father is unwilling to give, but that certain blessings cannot be bestowed without some preparatory delay.

The host of this belated traveller is a servant of God, who welcomes as a friend the man who has missed his way. He gives him shelter with cordial goodwill, and would give him that bread which cometh down out of heaven. But this he has not of himself; he must go forth to make request for it. The bread of life must be received as the gift of God.

Reasons for the delay of our Father, who wills to grant our request, but who holds us waiting at his threshold, may not all lie level to our understanding. This one at least is obvious: God has no more precious gift to bestow on his children than that they should possess words of life whereby those for whom they labour and pray may be saved. He will not grant this high privilege to any who do not value it aright, who ask it indolently or selfishly. Such a prayer must purify itself (as a river is cleansed in its flow) before it can be accepted by the Father. There must be an intense, a selfless, and a spiritual longing for spiritual gifts.

Having uttered this parable, Christ adds a further lesson touching that prayer which craves the gifts of the Spirit. (Luke 11:11-13.) When we plead for these the answer generally comes in an unlooked-for way. We ask bread, the Father seems to offer us a stone; we request a fish, does he not send us a serpent? We desire an egg, and that which is given to us bites like a scorpion. Prayer for spiritual endowments will in the first resort bring us very low; we shall be abashed and humbled; we shall be brought to the dust of contrition. And it may be that which was dear to us as a right eye, profitable as a right hand, must be taken away. To ask for the fullness of the Spirit may prove itself a costly undertaking. But if we are willing to pay the price, the blessing shall be ours.

'If ye then, being evil, know how to give good gifts unto your children, how much more shall your heavenly Father give the Holy Spirit to them that ask him' (Luke 11:13).

2

Our Lord spoke another parable, to this end, that men ought always to pray, and not to faint. (Luke 18: 1-8.) The incident which he pictured was such as might easily occur in the East. A woman, left a widow, was oppressed by a powerful neighbour or kinsman. He appropriated the farm or vineyard, left by the deceased man to the care of his wife for behoof of his children. The widow appealed to the judge, but the defrauder had been beforehand with her. He had offered, as we may safely infer, a substantial bribe for a decision to be given in his favour; so that, when the widow came crying for justice, she was driven away from the place of judgment.

But as often as she was ejected, so often she returned. Morning by morning she awaited the opening of the court, and was always the first to present her plea: 'Justice, my lord, justice.' This continued until the resolution of the judge began to weaken. He vociferates loudly, but it is mostly bravado; he speaks with a grimace of humour, but he feels deeply. He says: 'I neither fear God, nor regard men.' Methinks, he doth protest too much.

His conscience is beginning to stir. He is sensible of the meanness of his conduct; he knows that men look on him with disfavour, perhaps with contempt; a recognition of the high and reverend quality of righteousness, and of his obligation as the servant and minister of justice, oppresses him. He awakes to an acknowledgement of his duty. We may suppose that he throws back the bribe in the face of his tempter, and proceeds to give even-handed equity to the clamorous woman.

It is at this point - a very narrow point it is - that the thought of God finds place in this story. 'The righteous Lord loveth righteousness.' Justice and judgment are the foundation of Jehovah's throne. The Judge of all the earth will do right.

The widow in the parable represents the Church. Her children are defrauded of their inheritance, and she is in an agony on their account. She will dare anything for their sakes. Her resolution is indomitable, because it is sustained by love. She is willing to become a public spectacle, to enter into the most painful situations, to risk bodily peril for herself, if only she may retrieve the calamity of her children. And when she acts thus, God, rising from his throne, gives decree in her favour. The parable seems to speak of vengeance; what it does refer to is legal rectification - a cessation of the injury and a restoration of the right; shall not God do right to his own elect, which cry day and night unto him, though he bear long with them? I tell you that he will justify them speedily.

He bears long; he suffers long. 'God is patient,' says St Augustine, 'patient, because he is eternal.' But our hopes and fears are narrowed to this little space of time, and we implore him to make haste. 'Though the promise tarry, wait for it; it will not always tarry.' In some good hour, and that hour will be the divinely appointed season, the divine fiat shall go forth; God will interpose. We cannot fathom his reason for delay. They are good and necessary reasons; of this we may be sure. But possible delay in our receiving the answer to our prayers is always to be reckoned with. Therefore our Lord spoke this parable - 'to this end, that men ought always to pray and not to faint.'

Delay is not denial. The assurance of an answer to believing prayer is based on the character of God. He is 'a God of truth and without iniquity; just and right is he' (Deut 32:4). In prayer we may appeal to the divine righteousness. That, for example, is the force of the warrant which we bring when we pray in the Name of Jesus. In Christ the promises of God, how many soever they be, are all 'Yea.' Every promise is ours in Christ by an indefeasible right. We may plead each one with an authority like to that with which our glorified Saviour is vested. 'Fear not; only believe.'

This parable represents a mother praying for her children's welfare. Does it not cover the case of a Christian mother asking God to save her boys and girls? Is it not the fact that most of us who have come to Christ have found the way of life in answer to our mother's prayers?

A young man, during the Welsh Revival, was agonizing in a corner of a village chapel. After a time deliverance came to him. He lifted up a tear-stained face, and shouted, 'Well done, Mother!' In another village a woman, enfeebled and not able to attend the meetings, sat nightly at the door of her cottage as the congregation streamed up the village street. She was waiting to hear news of the homecoming of her boy. Night after night she asked: 'Has he come in?' Night after night the answer was: 'Not yet.' But one evening the neighbours crowded up the street to give her the welcome announcement: 'He is in!'

One has difficulty in making an absolute claim on God for the salvation of some for whom we have prayed. We must bow before the divine sovereignty. We may cherish a fervent hope that God will hear our prayer; but we cannot insist that he shall. But in the case of a Christian mother it is different. Her children are within the covenant which is ordered in all things and sure. The Christian family is, in some sense, a unit in the sight of God:

'The promise is unto you, and to your children, and to all that are afar off, even as many as the Lord our God shall call' (Acts 2:39).

The children of believing parents are in a class by themselves: because of their parents' faith they have a special claim upon God.

But the answer may be long of coming. We read, near the close of our Lord's ministry, that his brethren did not believe in him. (John 7: 5.) No doubt they were men of excellent character, but they had not committed themselves to the Saviour. In their uprightness they may not have been sensible of their need of redemption. Perhaps it was the Cross of Jesus that convinced them of their need. At all events, very soon after the death on Golgotha, we find them among the waiting saints in the Upper Room. But we think of Mary's prayers for them, and we think of our Lord's intercession. Yet the years passed, and they were still unbelieving when he breathed out his soul to God. Then the answer came. Does it not sometimes happen that a godly mother's prayers remain unanswered through long years of hope deferred? She may even pass from earth without any comfort of assurance in this matter. But the covenant holds.

Before our Lord passes from this parable he turns it toward the expected day of his return. 'The Spirit and the Bride say, Come.' The Church is looking upward, waiting for the appearance of the Son of Man from heaven; and scoffers are crying, Where is the promise of his coming? The Saviour seems to shade his eyes as he looks piercingly down the vistas of time: 'When the Son of Man cometh, shall he find faith on the earth?' He does not say that he will not, but he seems to imply that faith will be hard to come by in the days which precede his advent.

3

The Lord Jesus spoke another parable with reference to prayer. It has to do not with the intercession of a redeemed soul for those who are still in darkness, but with the supplication of a sinful man for forgiveness and acceptance.

'Two men went up into the temple to pray; the one a Pharisee, and the other a publican' (Luke 18:10).

'The Pharisee stood and prayed thus with himself.' This is not prayer; true prayer is the cry of a needy soul, but this man knows no lack - he is spiritually rich, and increased with goods, and has need of nothing. He is possessed of a satisfying righteousness, negative and positive. Negatively, he is not 'as this publican'; positively, he pays tithes of all that he has. With this tenuous covering of his guilty soul he is immeasurably content.

But the publican lifts up his heart to God. Bowed down under an appalling load of guilt, he dare not lift up his eyes to heaven, but beats upon his breast, crying: 'O God, be propitiated to me, the sinful one.' He cannot believe that any other son of Adam has sinned so grievously as he, the chief of sinners, has done. All his request is for pardoning mercy. Atonement for sin has been provided; for that he craves. It is as if he were making the cry of the penitent king his own: 'Purge me with hyssop, and I shall be clean: wash me, and I shall be whiter than snow' (Psalm 51: 7). Immediately, while he is yet praying, the answer comes: he is forgiven; he goes down to his house justified.

The chief instruction of this parable is, that a sincere prayer for pardon will be met and honoured without delay. One of those who listened to our Lord's discourse has cast this lesson into a doctrinal form:

'If we confess our sins, he is faithful and just to forgive us our sins, and to cleanse us from all unrighteousness' (1 John 1:9).

4

Luther, commenting upon the sacramental discourses preserved in St John's Gospel, writes:

'This is certainly the most choice and comfortable sermon that the Lord Christ uttered in this world... Moreover, herein are most forcibly grounded and settled (as nowhere else in the Scriptures) the true distinctive and chief articles of the Christian belief.'

What is perhaps the main doctrine insisted upon in these chapters is the worth and power of prayer; and especially this teaching regarding it, that all our prayers are to be presented to the Father in the name of Jesus, and that only in that name may we hope to receive an answer in peace. What our Lord most of all wished to convey to his disciples before he left them was his final instruction regarding the life of prayer.

1. What are we to understand by the expression, 'In my Name'?

(a) The name of the Lord Jesus is his self-manifestation - all that he has effected by word or act in this world of men. By faith we *abide in Christ* - we make our home in the revelation of the Father which our Lord has given. Therefore we are received into union with Christ in his relation to the Father, according to his own word: 'I in them, and thou in me' (John 17:23). The sphere of life which the children of faith now inhabit is 'Christ'. We share his wealth, we are vested in his glory, we are joint-heirs with him; all that the Father hath is ours in him. It is in him therefore that our prayers receive a meet answer.

(b) To us, living and abiding in Christ, all authority in heaven and on earth is communicated. When we draw near to God the Father, we present our supplications and intercessions in the name of the Only-begotten Son. The prayer-life in Christ acknowledges no frontier, it reaches out to a limitless dominion: '*Whatsoever* ye ask,' 'If ye shall ask *anything*.' There is but one invincible condition: we must ask in the name of

Jesus, in harmony with his Spirit, in obedience to his will, in fellowship with himself. Thus we become partakers with God in the regeneration of the world. Our prayers, inspired by the Holy Ghost, repeat the intercession of the Son of Man, once on earth, and now before the Throne. When the Divine Spirit intercedes within us, 'according to God' (Rom 8:27) it is *in Christ* that we pray.

(c) But as a man will not lend his name to any enterprise which does not approve itself to his mind, so our Lord Jesus Christ grants his name only to those causes with which he himself is identified. Therefore he says:

'If ye abide in me, and my words abide in you , ye shall ask what ye will, and it shall be done unto you' (John 15:7).

The sayings of Jesus confirm the renewed will, inflaming us with a holy energy to work the works of God. His words challenge us; they are the promises and the entreaties, the warnings and the rebukes, the precepts and exhortations of him whom we love to term 'Lord'. As we give heed to these, the word of Christ dwells richly in us. And the words of Christ, as the efflorescence of his very life, are himself.

To pray in the name of Jesus, therefore, is to pray in Christ.

2. In describing the prayer-life which is in

Christ, our Lord marks out three ways by which the supplicant may come to God. Each of them, however, bears this clear blazon, 'In my Name'.

(a) Our Lord begins by telling us, for our greater encouragement, that he himself holds authority to hear and answer prayer:

> 'Whatsoever ye shall ask in my name, that will I do, that the Father may be glorified in the Son. If ye shall ask me anything in my name, I will do it' (John 14:13,14).

'By these words,' says Luther, 'He gives us plainly to understand that he is the true Almighty God, equally with the Father.' This is undoubtedly implied - he who receives and answers prayer must himself be very God; but our Lord seems here rather to indicate his place on the Mediatorial Throne, his kingship in the realm of grace. He is about to pass into the Unseen; the land of far distances stretches cold and unwelcoming before the mind of the disciples; but, saith he, 'I shall be there, and when you come to the Father in my name, you come to me.' Our Brother is on the Throne, the Nearest of Kin will meet us on the threshold - we see God in the face of Jesus Christ.

(b) Again, we come by Jesus to the Father:

> 'I chose you... that whatsoever ye shall ask of the Father in my name, he may give it to you' (15:16).

It is not now the Son, but the Father, who receives the petition and grants the request. Sinners as we are, conscious of defilement, confessing our trespasses, we come by the new and living way which our High Priest has inaugurated for us in his flesh, with the name of Jesus on our lips and his blood sprinkled upon our hearts. We are accepted in the name of the Beloved. We stand in Christ; he is made of God unto us righteousness, sanctification and redemption. It is as if our Saviour took our prayers, presenting them to the Father as his own, making request in us, for us. Those prayers which we offer in the name of Jesus he has already presented on his own behalf. He has asked the Father that he may receive the nations for his inheritance and the uttermost parts of the earth for his possession; and he is able to communicate to his people the fruit of his intercession.

(c) Our union with the Father through Christ is so intimate that our Lord, contemplating our direct entrance into the Holiest, authorizes us to witness to his name before the Father:

'If ye shall ask anything of the Father, he will give it you in my name' (John 16:23).

It is as if the Father retained the name of Jesus, and we were permitted to go unaccompanied into the Sacred Presence, crying 'Abba, Father.' Jesus encourages his followers to enter on this hazard of faith by giving them the most animating assurance of their welcome:

'I say not unto you that I will pray the Father for you, for the Father himself loveth you' (John 16: 26-27).

Undoubtedly the Saviour will intercede for his people; he is unchangeably their Advocate before the Throne: the sweetest comfort vouchsafed to us in all our earthly journeyings is that he ever liveth to make intercession for us.

But in this crisis of his disciples' faith he is, for the moment, more anxious that they should concentrate attention on another privilege belonging to their divine inheritance:

'The Father himself loveth you, because ye have loved me, and have believed that I came forth from the Father' (16:27).

We do not come in our own right, but we are loved for our own sake. The Father is not unrighteous to forget our work of faith and labour of love and patience and hope, and he loves us because we have been true to his Son, have companied with him in all his temptations, and have borne his name unsullied through a mocking world. We come to the Father, in the name of Jesus, because the Father himself loveth us.

3. Our Lord reveals to us in these chapters a

three-fold efficacy of prayer in the name of Jesus.

We may name these fields of intercessional activity - Service for the Kingdom, Advancement in personal Holiness, a more intimate Knowledge of God.

(a) 'Verily, verily, I say unto you, He that believeth on me, the works that I do shall he do also; and greater works than these shall he do; because I go unto the Father. And whatsoever ye shall ask in my name, that will I do' (John 14:12,13). Our Lord is about to ascend from earth to the Right Hand of power, but his mighty works do not cease; they continue in still more glorious manifestations, though now they are accomplished through his Church. It does not appear as if our Lord, in speaking of *greater works*, were contrasting the rapid diffusion of the Gospel after his resurrection with the meagre results of his own ministry; he is rather comparing material wonders with the miracles of grace.

At his word the lame walked, the dumb spake, the lepers were cleansed, the eyes of the blind were opened; but under the preaching of the victorious cross and the broken grave, souls that were dead in sins are born into eternal life. No nature-miracle can for one moment be compared with the marvel of sins forgiven and lives renewed. And it is by prayer in the name of Jesus that these things are wrought.

(b) 'Ye did not choose me, but I chose you,

and appointed you, that ye should go and bear fruit, and that your fruit should abide; that whatsoever ye shall ask of the Father in my name, he may give it you' (John 15:16).

Fruit is for nourishment and delectation, therefore St Paul writes to the Church in Rome:

'That I might have some fruit in you also, even as in the rest of the Gentiles' (Rom 1:13).

In this sense the word is employed in the epitaph of Count von Zinzendorf, the founder of the *Unitas Fratrum*: 'He was ordained that he should bring forth fruit, and fruit that should remain.' But in the fifteenth chapter of John our Lord seems to use this word in a different sense. The fruit of the vine is the expression of its life, and this life robes itself in all those virtues which made the Son of Man so radiantly fair in the eyes of those who see wisdom.

'The fruit of the Spirit is love, joy, peace, long-suffering, kindness, goodness, faithfulness, meekness, self-control' (Gal 5:22,23).

Not one star in all this galaxy must be allowed to grow dim; all must shine with increasing lustre, until holiness be perfected in the fear of the Lord. And holiness is won by earnest and continuous prayer in the holy name of Jesus.

(c) 'In that day ye shall ask me nothing. Verily,

verily, I say unto you, If ye shall ask anything of the Father, he will give it you in my name. Hitherto have ye asked nothing in my name: ask, and ye shall receive, that your joy may be fulfilled. These things have I spoken unto you in parables: the hour cometh, when I shall no more speak unto you in parables, but shall tell you plainly of the Father' (16:23-25).

It is as if he said: 'I am going away. You will not henceforth be able to come to me in bodily presence, questioning me about many things - I go to the Father. But it is better so: it is expedient for you that I go away. Henceforth I will speak to you not in figures and comparisons drawn from material things, but in spiritual language. This teaching will pass through your own mind, and become a personal possession: it will bring to your knowledge heavenly things in a speech more apprehensive, more sure, than that of earth.'

Eye hath not seen, nor ear heard, neither have entered into the heart of man, the things which God hath prepared for those who love him - but they are being revealed by the Holy Spirit. St John, remembering these sayings of Christ, delivered them anew to his little children in Ephesus:

'Ye have an anointing from the Holy One, and ye know all things... And as for you, the anointing which ye received of him abideth in you, and ye need not that any one teach you; but as his anointing teacheth you concerning all things, and is true,

and is no lie, and even as it taught you, ye abide in
him' (1 John 2:20,27).

The loftiest privilege of the Christian faith is
that we should enter into the excellency of the
knowledge of Christ, daily becoming acquainted
with him in clearer recognition and ampler experience, learning daily and hourly the fullness of
his grace and the riches of his glory, until, in the
contemplation of his measureless mercy, we are
'lost in wonder, love and praise'. And it is by
prayer in the name of Jesus that we attain to this
most excellent knowledge.

All this, in the absence of Christ, and while he
tarries. The name of Christ, which signifies his
self-revelation, reminds us also that he has withdrawn himself from earth for a time. It is precisely
this absence which introduces us to those vast
fields of intercession which invite us to new acts
of communion with our Lord. When he returns
in the glory of the Kingdom, apart from sin, unto
salvation, prayer will give place to praise and
adoration. Until then, all our petitions express
themselves as a sigh for his appearing. 'The
Spirit and the Bride say, Come.' 'Come, Lord
Jesus, come quickly.'

'Ask, and ye shall receive,' said our Saviour,
'that your joy may be fulfilled' (John 16:24). The
depth of our prayerfulness is the measure of our
gladness.

CHAPTER TEN

THE HIGH-PRIESTLY PRAYER
(John 17)

'Put off thy shoes from off they feet, for the place whereon thou standest is holy ground.' No spot on earth is nearer heaven than the shaded recess in the valley of the Kidron, where our Lord and his disciples arrested their steps for a time on the way to Gethsemane. Melanchthon says:

'Nothing more dignified, nothing more holy, nothing more fruitful, nothing more pathetic has ever been heard in heaven or earth, than this prayer of the very Son of God.'

And another adds this testimony:

'This prayer is solitary among all the prayers of mankind, separated from all others by a perfect illumination, which is at the same time a perfect repose. It has no voice of confession, deprecation, supplication; no echo, however distant, of recognition of sin, no tone that it touched with a feeling of demerit or defect; only the certain consciousness, 'I have glorified thee on the earth; I have finished the work which thou gavest me to do.' There is no intimation of infirmity or entreaty for help; for self only one request, 'Glorify thy Son, that thy Son also may glorify thee.'

This witness is true. No words ever uttered in the audience of men are more divine than those of our Saviour's intercessory prayer. In this illustrious chapter - 'the sanctuary of the universe', it has been called - we see the glory of God streaming through the veil of flesh.

The late Dean Vaughan confessed that it was only with 'a painful effort' that he could nerve himself to read this prayer of intercession in public. The greatest expositors have scarcely dared to make its profound sentences the theme of their discourse.

Our Lord's Prayer of Consecration is indeed the sacredest shrine of Scripture, the Holiest of all. Yet it has been given for our instruction, and we may not turn from the consideration of it, even at the bidding of reverence. For it is doctrine as well as prayer. It is addressed to the minds of the disciples as directly as to the ear of God. All the varied discourse at the Supper Table is gathered together and certified in this priestly utterance. 'This prayer of Christ,' writes Calvin, 'was a sealing of the precious teaching, as well that it should be ratified in itself, as that it should create firm faith in his disciples.'

And many a soul has found comfort in a dark hour through these words. When John Knox, the Scottish Reformer, came to the brink of the silent river, he said to his wife: 'Go, read where I cast my first anchor.' She read the seventeenth chapter of St John's Gospel, after which he fell asleep.

Spener the Pietist also, though he had never ventured to preach upon this chapter, greatly loved it; as his end drew near, he asked those who surrounded his couch to read it aloud to him. When they had done so, he said, 'Again'; after that, at his renewed request, they read it a third time. Then he confessed that it seemed to him that the true understanding of this prayer transcends the measure of faith which the Lord is wont to impart to his disciples during their pilgrimage.

Here there are deeps beyond deeps and heights surmounting heights. We are constrained to say of these words what Job confessed with regard to the mysteries of nature:

'Lo, these are but the outskirts of his ways, and how small a whisper do we hear of him, but the thunder of his mighty deeds who can understand?' (Job 26:14)

This chapter falls into three sections, each distinguished by a special use of the Sacred Name - 'Father', 'Holy Father', 'Righteous Father'. Our Lord, speaking for himself, uses the simple word *Father* as no other can, for he is Son by absolute right. Afterwards, when he makes intercession for his disciples, he addresses the

Deity as *Holy Father* for he is the Author of holiness in those who believe. And at the close of the prayer, he speaks of God as *Righteous Father* for it is in righteousness that he has revealed himself to the world of men.

1

'These things spake Jesus, and lifting up his eyes to heaven, He said, Father, the hour is come; glorify thy Son, that the Son may glorify thee.' The Father is as near to Jesus as the disciples are; his presence is as manifest. Our High Priest presents himself to the Father, reporting the fulfilment of the task assigned to him, acknowledging as 'his own' those whom the Father had given him.

The Father had given to the Son, in the ages before time, a people of redemption. These he covenanted to call, redeem, and sanctify, in the shedding of his own blood: they were predestinated as his inheritance, his glory and joy.

With these there was granted to the Son power over all flesh, that he should give eternal life to those whom he had received. The fullness of the Spirit's grace, resting on the Son and ministered through him, was to be the divine agency effecting the new birth in those who should believe.

This new birth was to be the entrance of the redeemed on eternal life - a life like God's own - a life of holiness and truth, of growing conformity to the likeness of Christ. For 'this is life eternal, to know thee the only true God and him whom thou didst send, even Jesus Christ.'

Our Saviour claims the promised bestowment in the right of his obedience unto death. He does not supplicate, he requires (v 9, 15, 20); he does not implore, he wills (v 24). He anticipates his death, presenting his prayer with authority because of it: 'Father, the hour is come.' That hour which has been drawing near through unnumbered ages of measureless grace, is an hour of sorrow and dismay, of victory and rejoicing, an hour central in the history of the world and in the life of God. Already, in the Master's view, that hour has approached and gone. His life is rendered up with acceptance:

'I glorified thee on the earth, having accomplished the work which thou hast given me to do.'

He lifts up an unblemished sacrifice to God, and claims the promised reward.

The contrast between this prayer and that of Gethsemane, offered on the same evening and with only a brief space of time between, is startling. *Here* the outshining of the divine glory is so overpowering that the sharpness of death, the ignominy of the Cross, and even the agony of forsakenness are unheeded - it is as if they were already past.

There the unutterable anguish of the Sin-bearer seems to blot out of the heavens the light of the Father's face. In either case we are dealing with magnitudes that are greater than any measuring rod can mete - infinite love, unutterable pain. The difference seems to lie in this: in the one case our Saviour is gazing with undimmed eyes on the unveiled Presence, and his human heart rises in rapture, saying: 'Now come I to thee'; in the other, he has humbled himself to receive a prelibation of the bitter cup. 'Let this cup pass from me. The cup which the Father hath given me, shall I not drink it?'

As our Lord presents his finished work to the Father, he makes this one request:

'And now, O Father, glorify thou me with thine own self with the glory which I had with thee before the world was.'

The hour has come for the recall of the Ambassador from a distant country, the return of the Son to his ancestral home. The mission of the Eternal Word began 'before the world was' - his goings forth were from ancient days, from everlasting. In the divine prevision our Lord was foreordained to be a sacrifice before the foundation of the world (1 Pet 1:20); in the gift of the Father's love the Lamb of God was slain ere time had begun its course (Rev 13:8). Throughout all ages this high eternal covenant pointed forward to the fullness of the times when the Word became incarnate and the Son clothed himself in our nature. Bishop Westcott says concisely:

> 'Whatever men have found to kindle hope lies all in the few syllables: the Word became flesh; and I cannot conceive anything which can go beyond it.'

In becoming man our Lord humbled himself, became poor, laid aside the dignities and glories of his high estate, and came forth from God. Now, he is about to resume the divine mode of being, dwelling in the sweet immediacy of holy love with the Father, face to face in co-equal union.

In an attempt to explain the unexplainable the doctors of the Latin Church were accustomed to say that the Son went forth from the Bosom of God, without leaving it. While on earth, he was still in heaven (John 3:13; 12: 26; 14: 3; 17: 24). But in his coming there was privation, and the feeling of absence. Now he prays for a return to the full, unclouded fellowship of the eternal years: 'Glorify thou me with thine own self.' The sentence is pregnant: it implies the *presence* and the *possession* of God, without limit or restraint. The Son of Man returns to his eternal home.

In the 22nd verse the Saviour says:

'The glory which thou hast given me I have given unto them.'

In Christ we also are introduced into the Presence of God and are privileged to become possessors of his fullness. We are joint-heirs with Christ, and 'there is nothing alien in God'; 'God, even our own God, shall bless us.'

Here are some of the gifts which our Lord had during the years of his ministry bestowed upon 'his own' and which we also may receive out of his fullness, grace upon grace.

(a) *I have manifested thy name unto the men whom thou gavest me out of the world* (v 6). The Lord Jesus is the revelation of the Father. He is the effulgence of his glory and the express image of his person. The divine glory shone through our Lord's human vesture more and more clearly as his passion grew still more intense, until, on that night in which he was betrayed, he was able to say: 'He that hath seen me hath seen the Father.' (John 14:9).

b) *'The words which thou gavest me I have given unto them'* (v 8). This reference includes both the sayings and doings of the Lord Jesus, which, taken together, constitute the revelation of the Son in his unspotted holiness and unutterable love. To receive his 'words' is to receive himself.

(c) *While I was with them, I kept them in thy name, which thou hast given me; and I guarded them, and not one of them perished, but the son of perdition, that the Scripture might be fulfilled'* (v 12). The shadow of sin falls across the glory that fills that Upper Room. Until the end of all things, when God shall present the complete vindication of the moral government of the world, sin shall remain an insoluble mystery - sin in its permission and continuance.

All but the son of loss have been preserved from loss; they have been shielded under the prayers, the warnings, and the high example of their blessed Lord; walking in his footsteps they have not erred; through faith they have been guarded 'unto a salvation ready to be revealed in the last time' (1 Pet 1:5).

2

In the second division of this prayer the Saviour commends to the Father those who by gift and purchase are 'his own' (John 13:1). Six times at least in this short chapter the Lord Jesus repeats the words: 'Those whom thou hast given me.' Believers are inexpressibly dear to him as being the Father's gift; they are precious also because they are the subjects of his redeeming love. For them his petition is, that they may become holy. The sanctification which he implores on their behalf comes from the Name and Being of God, and consists principally in three articles: (a) that they may be kept from the evil that is in the world (v 11); (b) that they may be perfected together in love (v 21); and (c) that they may have their dwelling with him in regions unseen and eternal (v 24).

'Holy Father... make them holy.' These words are central to the second part of the Prayer of Intercession. They were uttered in confirmation of our Lord's petition that his people might be hallowed: 'For their sakes I sanctify myself, that they also may be sanctified in truth.'

1. 'Holy Father... make them holy.' Holiness has its ground in God. It is only in the measure in which we are assimilated to the Divine Nature that we are sanctified.

The holiness is inscrutable; it is of dazzling splendour; he dwells in light that is inaccessible and full of glory. We discern it only as we resign ourselves to its sacred influences; we are changed into its semblance only as we draw near.

(a) In our creation we are framed within the likeness of Deity. Our true bent is towards him who alone is holy. The consent of our manifold impulses aspires toward that harmony which characterizes the divine perfection. Upon each distinguishing virtue is imprinted the imperative of the rule of God: 'Be ye therefore perfect, even as your Father which is in heaven is perfect' (Matt 5:48).

(b) The natural craving for symmetry of character which belongs to us as our birthright is reinforced by the grace of the Holy Spirit who works in us to will and to do according to the Father's good pleasure. We advance as in a journey, we strive as in a contest, we toil towards an end; at last we come to the fullness of the perfect life.

One step more, and the goal receives us;
One word more, and life's task is done;
One toil more, and the cross is carried -
And sets the sun.

(c) The measure of this perfection is the full stature of the Christ.

In the beauty of his character our Lord has met the aspirations of the soul athirst for God, and has transcended them. All our loftiest ideals are fulfilled; yet this is only the beginning of the soul's itinerary towards God. The rule of the road is: 'He that saith he abideth in him ought himself also so to walk even as he walked.' And at every step we recognize some new trait of goodness in our adorable Master. Day by day, in our enlarging experience, he is, as it were, transfigured before us. The most glorious achievements of the saints are but the glancing radiance that falls from the white splendour of his renown. He towers above our attainments as the stars lift themselves above the hills, but our hopes soar upwards through vast regions of the spirit, defying extinction; for 'we know that if he shall be manifested, we shall be like him, for we shall see him as he is.'

2. Such is the holiness of Christ. What was the method of his sanctification? Only here does he speak explicitly of it. 'For their sakes,' he says, 'I sanctify myself.'

The root meaning of the word 'sanctify' is *consecrate*. One who is dedicated to God becomes, by the very necessity of his self-oblation to the thrice-holy One, himself holy.

Between the consecration of the Son of God and our own an important distinction is marked. 'Sanctify thou them,' he prays - we are sanctified through him. But he is the priest of his own consecration - 'I sanctify myself'. For he is not as we are. We are sinners; he is sinless. We are saved by grace; he is the Saviour. We are ignorant and erring; he is a High Priest chosen from among men in things pertaining to God. We are being sanctified through the Word; he is himself the Word which sanctifies.

And yet, in perfect harmony with this contrast, there is a parallelism between his self-consecration and ours. We have seen that holiness in us involves our being kept in the will of God, our being fulfilled in love, our being raised into the new life of the Spirit. In all these respects the Son of the Blessed, who is also Man of our manhood, affirms: 'I sanctify myself.'

(a) *The Lord Jesus held himself resolutely and unshakenly within the will of his Father.* In the beginning, as he has told us, the Father consecrated him and sent him into the world. His response was:

'Lo, I am come; in the volume of the book it is prescribed to me: I delight to do thy will, O my God; yea, thy law is within my heart' (Psalm 40: 7-8)

Commenting on these words, a New Testament writer presents this interpretation:

'By the which will we are sanctified through the offering of the body of Jesus Christ once for all' (Heb 10:10).

In his humiliation our Lord became obedient to law. He proceeded to honour the will of his Father, to fulfil the commission entrusted to him. From the beginning he foreknew that his way to the Throne lay through sacrifice. In spite of the natural shrinking of our human flesh from pain, in defiance of the solicitations of the evil one, he set his face, and went unswervingly down the appointed way of the holy Cross.

Now he stands at the crisis of his life of self-sacrifice. He came to our earth, that he might minister to the needy, and ministering give his life (Mark 10:45). So that actually he took our manhood, that he might lay it down. He became incarnate, that he might die. At last, the hour to which he has long been hastening has struck. Swiftly the Father will withdraw from his beloved Son the light of his Presence, the comfort of his strengthening arm.

Our Lord stands almost at the gate of the Olive Garden, where the anguish is to fall on him to the uttermost. The divine indignation against sin is about to be poured into a cup of trembling which he shall receive from the hand of the Father. Yet with calmness he confronts the hour of desolation as it is about to strike, and advances to greet the holy, acceptable, and perfect will of God. 'For their sakes, I sanctify myself.'

This joyful obedience was an essential element in the great reconciliation. 'It was not his suffering so much as his willingness to suffer that pleased the Father,' says Bernard of Clairvaux. In the same strain Calvin avers: 'The obedience of Christ is the most important circumstance of His death.' Almost to the same effect our Lord has said: 'Therefore doth my Father love me, because I lay down my life, that I may take it again' (John 10:17).

(b) *In this we see the final gift of love*. It was in love that our Saviour came into the world:

'Ye know the grace of our Lord Jesus Christ that, though he was rich, yet for your sakes he became poor, that ye through his poverty might become rich' (2 Cor 8:9).

All the path of his progress was strewn with the largesse that betokened his triumph. He gave royally, extravagantly, without measure or calculation - he gave all that Godhead could bestow. Now one thing only remains to him unyielded - his life. And this he is about to offer, as the completion of the divine gift of himself. To the last reserve of his being he yields himself to those who are his friends; so that they may say, as if they stood alone in the world: 'He loved me, and gave himself for me.'

He gave himself generously, lovingly, joyfully. He embraced the Cross; the day on which he confronted death amid its darkest terrors was the day of the gladness of his heart. His divine charity in resistless flood overleapt the last barrier that would impede its progress, and poured itself out over the world in torrents of sovereign compassion. It is evident that even as our Lord was uttering this calm Prayer of Intercession the storm-filled petitions of the 22nd Psalm was pulsing through his mind in a strong undercurrent of thought and feeling (cf.: Psalm 22:22 with John 17:6,26). Yet how completely is the storm brought to a hushed serenity within the divine quietude. The psalm of the breaking heart has become a song in the night, as when a holy solemnity is kept, and gladness of heart as when one goeth with a melody to come into the mountain of the Lord, to the Rock of Israel.

In the Palace of Versailles there is a magnificent gallery dedicated 'to all the glories of France'. There is a long succession of battle-pieces, each one commemorating a triumph. The victorious generals are represented, for the most part, in some safe position on the field, in immaculate clothing, with untarnished lace and unruffled plumes. Far off one sees the baleful light of flaming towns; at a considerable distance the blast of artillery is depicted and the clash of opposing squadrons. To all this conventional art there is one exception. A great fight has been won, but at a fearful price; and now the victors are bringing home to its last resting-place the body of the dead leader. The lifeless form is supported on horseback by two dragoons, the white face is turned to the sky, and behind, the soldiers, with drooping heads, march in pained silence. Victory has been achieved, but the leader's life is forfeit.

It was only by uttermost self-sacrifice that the world was redeemed, only by uttermost self-sacrifice shall it be saved. 'For their sakes,' as he opens his hands to receive the rending nails; 'for their sakes,' as he bares his soul to the pitiless tempest, when all God's waves and billows pass over him; 'for their sakes, I sanctify myself.'

(c) But the death of the Leader of God's embattled host, although the forfeit of the war, was not the end. It is Christ that died; yea, rather, that is risen again, and is become the firstfruits of earth's full harvest. Accordingly, we find that *our Lord here is consecrating himself for entrance on his heavenly ministry.*

Jesus of Nazareth, girt with the simple purity of his nature and apparelled in the beautiful garments of his perfected obedience, stands on the threshold of his heavenly ministry. The path which led to that high office had stooped to the portals of the grave. Already, in this final consecration of his Person and Work, he has saluted and virtually endured the Cross. In surrendering himself to death he has, as it were, already died. He has forded the brook by the way, and now has his dwelling in the eternal light. Listen to his own words: 'Father, I have finished the work which thou gavest me to do... Now I am no more in the world... I come to thee... That which thou hast given me, I will that, where I am, they also may be with me.' Thus our Lord's consecration bears him into heaven. He had been pressing forward to this priestly ministry, not only during his earthly years, but also from of old, even from everlasting.

He had set his face towards Jerusalem that, having died, he might rise again, and so communicate to men his own deathless life. The resurrection of Christ is the true term of his life in the flesh. For it was in his rising from the dead, and in his clothing himself with a spiritual body, that the human Sonship of the Eternal Word was

fulfilled, according to the inspired sentence:
'Thou art my Son; this day have I begotten thee'
(Acts 13:33). And in this perfection of holy Manhood he is the figure of the ransomed Church, the First-born among many brethren:

> For me, Lord Jesus, thou hast died,
> And I have died in thee.
> Thou'rt risen; my bands are all untied,
> And now thou liv'st in me.
> When purified, made white, and tried,
> Thy glory then for me.'

This new life into which the Redeemer leads his people is a life where reconciliation is perfected and victory is secured. It is a life lived in heavenly places, enriched by the bestowment of the Holy Spirit, and powerfully wrought upon by the intercession of Jesus Christ.

3. In those particulars in which our Lord consecrated himself to his high office of mediation the believer discovers the method of his own sanctification.

It is in the virtue of Christ's overcoming that he intercedes for us:

'Holy Father, keep them in thy name which thou hast given me... keep them from the evil.'

This prayer, offered as of right by our glorified Redeemer, surrounds us as with a wall of defence. Into this sanctuary the enemy and the avenger cannot come. Dwelling within it, we are free from the noise of alarms, from the fear of failure and falling:

'He will not suffer thy foot to be moved; he that keepeth thee will not slumber. Behold, he that keepeth Israel shall neither slumber nor sleep... The Lord shall keep thee from all evil; he shall keep thy soul. The Lord shall keep thy going out and thy coming in, from this time forth, and for evermore' (Psalm 121).

(a) *It is a prayer for daily shelter within the will of God.* 'Holy Father, keep them... keep them from the evil.'

Life is dangerous in the extreme; its ways are perilous. An unguarded moment may bring a lifetime's regret, an unchecked desire may precipitate a shattering fall. The possibility of lasting failure lurks within us in our unsanctified impulses, surrounds us on every hand in the concourse of assailing temptations, and confronts us terribly in the direct assault of a personal evil spirit. But God is able to keep us from falling, and to present us faultless before the presence of his glory with exceeding joy. He is able to uphold in the safe ways of his direction even our weak, wayward feet.

There is a touching expression at the close of St John's First Epistle. All through the argument of that great doctrinal treatise the aged apostle has been summoning his little children to a strenuous war within. Life is a conflict, keen even to agony. Every mental power must be engaged, force must be intensified to the last degree, all the faculties, knit in stern accord, must be strained to the last point of effort. But at the close the trustful soul, in the full surrender of faith, flings itself in entire repose into the arms of Christ: 'He that was begotten of God keepeth him' (1 John 5:18).

(b) *It is a prayer that love may be made perfect.* Love to Christ first, then to his people, and finally to those who are ready to perish, but for whom the Saviour died. Love made perfect is holiness in the highest degree.

'I in them, and thou in me, that they may be made perfect in one; and that the world may know that thou didst send me, and lovedst them, even as thou hast loved me.'

The love of God was perfected towards us in the Cross of our Lord Jesus Christ; and as in faith and obedience we dwell there, that love is perfected in us. We stand in wonder and praise in the presence of this great mystery, the pained love of God; we open our hearts to receive it, we welcome its gracious influences, our cold hearts are kindled in its sacred flame - we 'love his love'. Dr Griffith Thomas, in a recent volume, quotes a sentence from Dr Whipple, Bishop of Minnesota, to the effect that for thirty years he had endeavoured to see the face of Christ in the countenances of those with whom he disagreed. That is the true spirit of love, to cherish the unthankful and the evil, to esteem others better than ourselves, to rejoice in the discovery of God's favour towards those with whom we differ.

(c) *Lastly, this is a prayer for fellowship with Christ in heavenly places.* 'Father, I will that they also whom thou hast given me be with me where I am.' This petition will be answered in it fullness in the heavenly state; it is being answered daily in the gift of a heavenly experience. Life is a continuous following in the footsteps of the Risen Lord. We dwell with him in his resurrection; we are shielded and strengthened by his most potent intercession; we are partakers with him in the promise of the Father, and are with him enriched by spiritual gifts; we wait in fellowship with him for the glad hour of his return. Christ and his people are united in such firm bonds that they shall never be sundered. Blaise Pascal prayed in an hour of great spiritual exaltation:

'Jesus Christ! Jesus Christ! Jesus Christ! I have renounced him, I have fled from him, I have separated myself from him; may I never be separated from him again!'

Now this, says our Lord, is being sanctified *in truth.* Not 'by the truth' as the instrument of our sanctification - that is spoken of in verse 17 - but here, in verse 19, the Saviour asks for our thorough, perfected, and complete sanctification. Let St Paul interpret for us those awe-inspiring words:

'The God of peace himself sanctify you wholly; and may your spirit and soul and body be preserved entire, without blame, at the presence of our Lord Jesus Christ. Faithful is he that calleth you, who also will do it -'

Now to our God whose power can do
More than our wants or wishes know,
Be everlasting honour done
In all the Church, through Christ, the Son.

In Rubens' famous cartoon 'The Triumph of Religion' the chariot of the truth is borne onward resistlessly. All forces that make for unhappiness or which tend to evil are led in captivity behind it: hunger, and sickness, and war, and the evil one himself, follow in chains. But on the car there are only two figures - Faith and Love. Faith has flung her arms round the gaunt, unshapely cross of unhewn wood, whereas Love is standing erect, lifting on high a radiant cup of blessing. This, in the view of the painter, is pure religion and undefiled - Faith embracing the cross, and Love bestowing benediction. Had I been a painter, I think I should have added a third figure - that of

Hope, with the day-star upon her brow, looking upwards for his appearing, and whispering, her lips tremulous with emotion: 'It is not yet made manifest what we shall be. We know that, if he shall be manifested, we shall be like him, for we shall see him as he is' (1 John 3:2).

Archbishop Leighton, giving charge to the clergy of his diocese, conjuring them to perfect their holiness in the fear of the Lord, anticipated a reflection which might arise in the minds of some of those whom he addressed. This is what he wrote:

'But you will possibly say, What does he himself that speaks these things to us? Alas, I am ashamed to tell you. All I dare say is this: I think I see the beauty of holiness, and am enamoured of it, though I attain it not; and howsoever little I attain, would rather live and die in the pursuit of it, than in the pursuit, yea, in the possession and enjoyment, though unpurified, of all the advantages that this world affords. And I trust, dear brethren, you are of the same opinion, and have the same desire and design, and follow it both more diligently and with better success.'

3

It is in righteousness that God makes himself known as Father to the world of men. It is as Christ's Father that he allows us to call him by that endearing name, and Christ is the Right-eous One. This expression, which recurs so often in the New Testament, is borrowed from the passion-song of the Servant of Jehovah (Isa 53: 11).

Righteous in all his ways as the Suffering Messiah is, it is particularly because he has come under the Father's mandate to magnify the law and make it honourable, to restore that which he had not taken away, and to become sin for us though he knew no sin, that he is styled by the Evangelical Prophet 'Jehovah's Righteous Servant'. It is as the Sin-bearer, the stainless Sufferer, the atoning Lamb, that he is revealed to a world of sinners guilty and condemned. There is one Lawgiver who is able to save, One who has met the challenge and satisfied the claims of the avenging law, who is himself 'just and the Justifier' of the ungodly. He - he himself, in his doing and his dying - is the propitiation for our sins, and not for ours only, but also for the whole world.

Earlier in this prayer, the Saviour said: 'I pray for them: I pray not for the world, but for those whom thou hast given me' (v 9). This particular request he makes for 'his own' - that they may be holy. The world cannot be partaker in his intercession at this point; but afterwards he will intercede for them. Two things he will ask - that they may believe (v 21) and that they many know (v 23). He asks that they may believe in his divine mission, and that they may know the love of God toward them to be as the love which he bears to the Son.

(a) *'That the world may believe that thou didst*

send me.' The object of saving faith is variously indicated in the New Testament. Sometimes we are commanded to believe the words which our Saviour has spoken, at other times we are enjoined to believe in his name - his self-manifestation on earth. Again, we are invited to trust in his person; but always this act of saving faith terminates in God. All these modes of belief are signified in this brief sentence: 'That the world may believe that thou didst send me.' We trust himself, because of the life he lived, the works he accomplished, the words he spoke; and more than all, because he has come bearing a divine commission: 'My Father sent me,' he says, 'and I am come.' Thus the faith that saves is ultimately faith in the Father of our Lord Jesus Christ, and our Father.

(b) *'That the world may know that thou didst send me, and lovedst them, even as thou lovedst me.'* Faith becomes assurance, trust brightens into knowledge. Vinet asserts that the full assurance of faith is not the belief that we are saved, but that we are loved.

In its initial faith is simply faith: 'faith unformed' the Reformers styled it; 'naked faith' said the devout churchman of the Middle Ages. 'Faith alone saves,' protested Melanchthon, 'but the faith that saves is not alone.' Yet in the act of affiance whereby the soul is united to Christ, it seems to be alone:

Nothing in my hand I bring,
Simply to thy Cross I cling.

A singular reliance on Christ is the primary act of saving faith. This is, as the fathers of the Secession were accustomed to say, 'a venturesome believing.'

But when faith creates experience, knowledge is the fruit of this act of affiance: 'We know whom we have believed.' And in the knowledge of him who is our Saviour we know that he has come as the witness of a love which passes knowledge, and which the strongest faith can only feebly grasp:

'That the world may know that thou didst send me, and lovedst them, even as thou lovedst me.'

Behold, what manner of love!

So near, so very near to God;
I cannot nearer be;
For in the person of his Son,
I am as near as he.

So dear, so very dear to God;
I cannot dearer be;
The love wherewith he loves the Son,
Such is his love to me.

And now, in order that the world in all its

history may *believe* and *know*, the Saviour carries the burden of this marvellous prayer right to the bounds of time:

'O righteous Father, the world knew thee not, but I knew thee, and these knew that thou didst send me. And I have made known unto them thy name, and will make it known; that the love wherewith thou lovedst me may be in them, and I in them.'

Our Lord came to this earth, not merely to save those who were lost, but to reveal the Father. In the ages before his advent, men had become familiar with the thought of the divine holiness, goodness, and truth. But the power and passion of his love could not be made known until in human nature he had confronted the sin that marred our peace, had assumed our guilt, and died our death. The Father gave his Son to die; the Spirit sealed him for his atoning sacrifice, and the Son came, laying his life down of himself. The feelings of Abraham as he stood by the altar of Moriah, unsheathing the knife to slay his only son, Isaac, whom he loved, present us with what is perhaps the nearest Old Testament figure of the suffering love of God, when he hid his face from the Beloved and was pleased to put him to grief.

The divine righteousness was known to the fathers. Justice and judgment, they said, are the foundation of the eternal Throne. The ways of the Lord are right: whatever he doeth is according to equity and truth. In his sovereign procedure there is no shadow cast by turning. His kingly titles are 'Faithful' and 'True', and in righteousness is fully disclosed. Jehovah had sworn by himself that at any cost, even in the death of his dear Son, he would break the power of sin. This he has done by judging sin in the death of the Lord Jesus. 'Through the knowledge of himself shall my righteous Servant make many righteous; and he shall bear their iniquities' (Isa 53:11).

The holiness of God has been made the theme of age-long praise. The prophets sang the trisagion (Isa 6:3) and the Psalmist re-echoed the strain (Psalm 99:3, 5, 9). The law also commanded the attainment of a purity like to that of God (Lev 19:2). Now, however, through all the Christian years, in the experience of all saints, the measure of the divine holiness is seen to pass beyond our human reach. It shines infinitely far above us, yet it is the goal to which we aspire. More and more, as we apprehend the surpassing perfection of the Holy One, we are changed into the same likeness, from glory to glory, in the presence and by the Spirit of the Lord.

CHAPTER ELEVEN

IN THE OLIVE GARDEN
(Luke 22:39-53)

'Put off thy shoes from off thy feet,' said the Lord to Moses, when he turned aside to see the bush that burned and was not consumed; 'the place whereon thou standest is holy ground.' One scarcely dares speak of Gethsemane and the midnight conflict, where our Redeemer agonised and overcame. Angels may have gathered round in awful reverence to gaze upon the suppliant Saviour, 'who in the days of his flesh, having offered up prayers and supplications with strong crying and tears unto him that was able to save him out of death, and having been heard for his godly fear, through he was a Son, yet learned obedience by the things which he suffered' (Heb 5: 7,8); but the very chiefest apostles could not endure to watch with their Lord one hour.

St Luke tells us that Jesus, having left the Upper Room, 'went, as his custom was, unto the Mount of Olives; and the disciples also followed him.' When he came to Jerusalem, to celebrate the great festivals, Gethsemane was, apparently, his resting-place for the night (Luke 21:37). He did not remain in the city, partly because he loved the simplicities of nature; partly, it is possible, because he was a poor man, and could not meet the cost of lodgings within the walls; but chiefly, we may suppose, because he desired privacy for prayer. How often, when the disciples had drawn their mantles round them and were pillowing their heads on the gnarled root of some olive tree, may not our Lord have watched and wept! We can imagine his fixed gaze, as the marble towers of the temple shone in the moonlight, and the heedless city slept, while the day of visitation was shaking out its swiftly running sands.

'O Jerusalem, Jerusalem, which killest the prophets, and stonest them that are sent unto her, how often would I have gathered thy children together, even as a hen gathereth her chickens under her wings, and ye would not!' (Luke 13:34).

May not ejaculations such as these, mingled with 'tears' and enforced with 'strong crying' have often interpreted the Saviour's silent communing with his Father?

There is a surprising contrast between the serenity of our Lord's High-Priestly Prayer and the overwhelming distress that shook his soul in Gethsemane's agony. He was sorrowful, exceeding sorrowful, sorrowful even unto death; he was greatly amazed and sore troubled; consternation possessed his spirit. Two things had come to pass: in the Upper Room he had said: 'The prince of the world cometh, and he hath nothing in me'; and in the Valley of the Kidron he had prayed: 'Father, the hour is come.'

That hour, foreordained through all the eternities, an hour of anguish and dread, had darkened upon the soul of the Messiah and Satan entered into the darkness, to assail the suffering Saviour with all the malice and craft of hell. The Captain of our salvation chose his battleground with judgment. In this place of prayer, hallowed by numberless seasons of communion with his Father, he will meet the adversary and withstand the shock of his onset. Our Redeemer did not shun the grasp of death: 'To die is but to fall asleep, on the kind arms of God'; nor was he greatly afraid of pain; it is his strength that has enabled the martyr saints to tread the lion and the adder underfoot. But soul and spirit recoiled from the doom of sin, due to mankind, and accepted by the Surety.

The word which he employs, 'this cup' (Luke 22:42), has reference, we believe, to the words with which he instituted the Feast of Remembrance: 'This is my blood of the covenant which is shed for many unto remission of sins' (Matt 26:28). The cup betokens his sacrificial offering for the sins of men. To us it offers heaven's richest benediction; to him it brought unutterable pain.

> Death and the curse was in our cup;
>   O Christ, 'twas full for thee!
> But thou hast drained the last drop;
>   'Tis empty now for me:
> That bitter cup,
> Love drank it up;
>   Now blessing's draught for me.

According to the First Gospel, which gives us the most consecutive account of our Lord's conflict in the Olive Garden, Jesus offered two distinct prayers - the second one repeated and prolonged. The first is given by St Matthew in these words: 'O my Father, if it be possible, let this cup pass away from me: nevertheless, not as I will, but as thou wilt' (Matt 26:39).

The Saviour asks if there may not be some other way of deliverance for mankind than that which exacts a measureless ransom price. From of old the Father has been devising means whereby his banished should not be expelled from him. Is this the only way that infinite wisdom can discover? Is salvation impossible to men on any other terms? The very question, coming from the Saviour's lips at such a time, speaks to us of the unfathomable mystery of the atoning sacrifice of the world's Redeemer. Even then, he, passing within the edge of the storm-cloud, acknowledges the transcendent virtue of the Cross.

The silence of the Father, or it may be his whisper within, reveals to the stricken Suppliant that there is no other way. Therefore, this first petition needs no longer to be offered, for it has been already laid within the blessed Will: 'Not as I will, but as thou wilt.' 'The cup which the Father hath given me,' he adds, 'shall I not drink it?' He takes it 'with a hand that trembles greatly,' yet he takes it 'lovingly', and will drain it to the dregs.

The prayer that now falls with insistence from his lips is a cry for strength:

'O my Father, if this cannot pass away, except I drink it, thy will be done.'

It is active obedience, not mere acquiescence, that he is learning in this storm of pain. He prays that he may be enabled *to do* the will of his Father; to this end he pleads that he may be saved out of death. He is in the throes of an appalling conflict, where death, the last enemy, now reinforced by the prince of evil himself, is contending with him for the mastery. Our Redeemer's spirit and soul are unshaken, but his physical force is weakened in the greatness of his way. To human sensitiveness it might appear as if he must fail in the hour of battle, as if his alliance with our manhood would force him to renounce the due reward of his pain and toil. 'Thy will *be done*,' he prayed: he passionately craved that he might be enabled to perform it -

'And there appeared unto him an angel from
heaven, strengthening him. And being in an agony,
he prayed more earnestly: and his sweat became
as it were great drops of blood falling down upon
the ground' (Luke 22:43,44).

Poets and painters have endeavoured to de-
pict the manner in which this succouring angel
conveyed the comfort of God. It has been suggested by one that the angel brought a personal
word of encouragement from the Father; by
another, that he reminded our Saviour of the
provisions of the covenant enacted before time
began; by a third, that he disclosed the significance of the atoning death; another represents
the angel as striking the harp of God and sound-
ing forth the anthem of those who stand by the
shores of the crystal sea redeemed, of those who
worship the Lamb that was slain.

Possibly all that the angel was commissioned
to do in this case, as in others (1 Kings 19:5-8;
Matt 4:11), was to renew the bodily strength of
our Daysman, exhausted in the strain and travail
of his mighty work of redemption. However it
may have been, we can all share with Dr John
Duncan his burning desire to have intercourse in
the realms of glory with 'the angel who came
down to strengthen my Lord in his agony in the

garden'. 'I have a wonderful affection,' he would say, 'for that angel.'

For the second time our Saviour rises from his agony of prayer, to bend over the slumbering forms of his disciples. Perhaps nowhere else, even in the life of Jesus, can we discover a nobler example of love forgetting its own great need in solicitude for the welfare of others.

'Backward and forward thrice he ran,' not so much to be solaced by human sympathy, though it had been a comfort to him to know that these beloved ones were near when his agony befell, as to bring to them the succour of God wherewith he himself had been sustained. Then he returned and flung himself again upon the trampled grass, saying the same words: 'O my Father, if this cannot pass away, except I drink it, thy will be done.' Ere long the victory was given; the powers of hell were broken, the dragon of the pit was crushed under the Redeemer's conquering heel. 'Oh my soul,' he might have said with the Hebrew prophetess, 'thou hast trodden down strength.'

Returning to his disciples, he said to them, as a mother might: 'Sleep on now, and take your rest.' He knew that they were sleeping for sorrow; he understood that the flesh was weak - he himself was touched with the feeling of their infirmity. He sat beside them, with the glory of God shining on his brow (cf. John 18:6), until the gleam of torches in the valley below told that the betrayer was at hand. Then he roused his followers, saying: 'Arise, let us be going' - let us go to meet them. One opportunity had passed unused, never to be recovered - they had failed to watch with Christ one hour in the Garden. The appeal to share his Gethsemane will not return: as regards this, they may sleep on and take their rest. But another field of witness is opening before them: they are now called to testify to Jesus before priests and rulers; they may even be privileged to die with him. Gethsemane lies behind, Calvary confronts us: 'Arise, let us be going.'

CHAPTER TWELVE

'FATHER, FORGIVE THEM'
(Luke 23:33-34)

The ignominy of the arrest, the trials and evil-questionings are over. The cross-beam is laid on shoulders bruised and torn with the leaded scourge, and the Sufferer goes forth bearing his reproach. Weakened with pain, he sinks under the load. Simon of Cyrene, coming up at that moment, is impressed to share the grim burden. So the sad procession comes to Golgotha.

The cross-beam was probably laid on the ground, and our Lord stretched upon it. The nails were driven through his hands, and an iron spike pierced his feet. In the blinding agony that followed, instead of the maniacal curses the Roman soldiers were accustomed to hear on such occasions, the tender tones of the Blessed One, supplicating pardon for his murderers, fell on their ears. Well might the centurion bear witness: 'Certainly, this was a righteous man. Truly this was a Son of God' (Luke 23:47; Matt 27:54).

'Father' - this is the first word uttered from the Cross. Our Lord is going into a darkness deeper than human despair, into a desolation which none of his people can ever know; but he goes trustfully, relying securely on that name on which Jehovah had caused him to hope. He advances to meet the doom of our sin as a loving child will hasten to greet his father, who comes to reward and bless. 'I am not alone,' he is able still to say: 'the Father is with me.'

The immediate reference of this prayer is to the soldiers, the unquestioning instruments of Roman justice. Truly, they knew not what they did. In all likelihood they had no knowledge of the career of the prophet of Galilee, nor had they watched the course of the trial, endeavouring to sift truth from falsehood. This was to them an ordinary malefactor, condemned by the processes of law to expiate his crimes upon the Cross. 'Father, forgive them,' prayed our Master; 'they know not what they do.'

May we widen the reference, taking it as inclusive of the Jewish nation, its rulers and the body of the people? Simon Peter, in Solomon's porch, may have had this prayer in his mind when he addressed in these terms the worshippers clustering round:

'Ye denied the Holy and Righteous One, and asked for a murderer to be granted unto you... and now, brethren, I wot that in ignorance ye did it, as did also your rulers' (Acts 3:14,17).

It is hard to think that Annas and Caiaphas, and

others of their faction, did not possess an inward conviction that Jesus was all that he professed to be. The rulers seem to have known that this was the very Christ. Yet the enormity of their guilt in compassing his death was hidden from them: they were able to understand only in the most fragmentary way all that their action involved. And the love of Jesus finds in this an argument for the bestowal on them of the riches of grace. No sinner is able in this life fully to comprehend the significance of his own iniquity. Would he be able to commit sin if he did? Can any one who is not a devil deliberately say: 'Evil, be thou my good'?

In this view, therefore, the prayer of Jesus reaches out to all mankind. His requests for his own are within his covenant of priesthood, and are infallibly granted. This (if we may make the distinction) is the supplication of One who was in all things like unto ourselves, who breathes out love and pity even under the strokes of the hammer and the first overwhelming sharpness of the Cross. We cannot draw from it the conclusion that all men shall be eternally saved: but in this supplication of the Lamb of God we learn to pray. We not only forgive those who may have injured us, we unfeignedly desire that they shall receive the pardoning grace of God.

This prayer of the dying Lord was harmonious with the course of his life; and we have his constant example to guide us in our prayers for pardon to those who have done us wrong:

'For hereunto you were called: because Christ also suffered for you, leaving you an example, that ye should follow his steps: who did no sin, neither was guile found in his mouth: who, when he was reviled, reviled not again; when he suffered, threatened not; but committed himself to him that judgeth righteously' (1 Pet 2:21-23).

We should always cherish a spirit of love and forgiveness, being ready at any moment to let that mind of charity express itself in word or act of mercy. St Paul exhorts the Colossian believers to 'put on Christ', and he draws out the particulars of that sacred investiture thus:

'Put on therefore, as God's elect, holy and beloved, a heart of compassion, kindness, humbleness of mind, meekness, long-suffering; forbearing one another, and forgiving each other, if any man have a complaint against any; even as the Lord forgave you, so also do ye' (Col 3:12,13).

It is most fitting that we should add in our own case the palliative our Lord offered with regard to the soldiers: 'they know not what they do.' For any offence against us is not a clear contravention of justice. There is in us so much to justify any hostile judgment on the part of those who are not well-affected towards us. Our character is tarnished with defects of various kinds, which mitigate the severity of the offence committed against us; and in the very article in which we protest against blame, we are found open in measure to hostile criticism. If those who impugn us had a clearer vision they would discern much that is now hidden from their eyes, and their bitter estimate would be softened. They would be able to discount our shortcomings, and appraise with a just valuation our efforts to live worthily. In the meantime, let us commit ourselves to him that judgeth righteously, and if any one shall have wrought us evil, let us pray: 'Father, forgive them.'

It is the dying Christ who asks the Father to grant forgiveness to those who crucify him and put him to an open shame. It is in the death of our Lord Jesus that forgiveness comes from God to sinners of Adam's race. It is his blood that cleanseth us from all sin.

> Do thou with hyssop sprinkle me,
> I shall be cleansed so;
> Yea, wash thou me, and then I shall
> Be whiter than the snow.

CHAPTER THIRTEEN

'WHY HAST THOU FORSAKEN ME?'
(Matthew 27:46)

Our Lord has made intercession for his murderers, has rescued from the second death the soul of the penitent robber, has commended his mother to the care of the beloved disciple; now he enters on this last dread conflict. Darkness falls upon the cross, veiling the agonies of the Sufferer from unsympathetic eyes. And the Father hides his face from the Son; it pleased the Lord to bruise him; he hath put him to grief.

Immanuel, the bearer of our sins, has entered the presence of the All-holy, and stands, as it were, before the Judgment Throne. He who knew no sin was made sin for us. He carries our sinfulness into the light of Jehovah's countenance, taking our guilt upon himself and making the turpitude of our sin his own. The divine lightnings smite the Sufferer; an end is made of sin and the transgression is finished. And Jesus cries: 'My God, my God, why hast thou forsaken me?' God cannot look upon sin, and our Lord has assumed our iniquity in so far as it was possible for him to do this without personal culpability.

This cry of desolation is the opening prayer of

Psalm 22. It is, no doubt, the poignant experience of a suffering saint of the olden time. It is possible that David, climbing the slopes of Olivet with dust-covered head and unsandalled feet, fleeing from his unnatural son and his rebellious subjects, uncrowned, dethroned, and fugitive, may have first uttered this bitter lament. But as his meditations ran clear, the Psalmist saw in his own grief the foreshadowing of a more appalling distress; he found himself walking in the appointed path of the Messiah.

It has been suggested by some expositors that the Lord Jesus may have rehearsed in spirit the verses of this Psalm, and that its closing words - 'He hath done it' - may have given form to the Saviour's shout of triumph - 'It is finished.'

The Psalmist first encourages himself in God, the Holy One, who is the very truth, and cannot deny himself. Afterward he reaffirms his lifelong confidence in him who is the worship of his Israel. On this twofold ground of assurance he poises his prayer, which beats up through the darkness into the presence of the Eternal. In the crisis of his agony, a foregleam of morning shoots through the shroud of night. 'Yea, from the horns of the wild oxen - thou hast answered me.' From this time the Psalm wings its way into the unshadowed light.

'Why hast thou forsaken me?' We may take this interrogation in two ways. First, as a challenge to the divine righteousness. Why should he who knew no sin be smitten? Why should this one whose faith had never faltered be permitted to die in darkness? Why should the Son, who always did the things which pleased the Father, be forsaken in his direst need? The very prayer gives a verdict. There must be a victorious issue for such a one out from among the snares of death, the pains of hell. The cloud will break, and the eternal glory shine through.

Or we may take it thus. There was in our Lord's mind, even when he was enduring the wrath of God due to us for sin, a sense of mystery. As Son of Man, feeling and thinking under conditions suitable to our manhood, the meaning of the vicarious sacrifice may, in that hour of utter darkness, have seemed to him not wholly clear. For the atonement is the revelation of all the mysteries which surround us. It sends its piercing light into the recesses of the divine nature, and it illumines the deep places of the human spirit.

Or, it may be, this cry has a retrospective force, as if we should translate it: 'My God, my God, why didst thou forsake me?' The darkness is passing, the cloud of dereliction melts into the light of heaven, the battle with principalities and powers is ended. And just before the exceeding great cry, 'It is finished,' goes ringing through earth and heaven and hell, our Saviour turns in love to his Father to ask: 'Why didst thou forsake me?'

It is noticeable, however, that in the midnight of his pain our Lord does not employ the word 'Father'. He has done so before. He will do so again; but in this moment the sweetness of the Father's love has been withdrawn. And Jesus rests on the covenant - the covenant of eternity, ordered in all things and sure. 'My God, my God, why hast THOU forsaken me?' Feelings may ebb with the tides, but the rock unshaken remains, the eternal truth, the faithfulness of God. It is firm as Jehovah's throne, it is steadfast as his Name. The faith of our Redeemer is vindicated, and now he declares in words which he had taken up into his High-Priestly Prayer:

'I will declare thy name unto my brethren: in the midst of the congregation will I praise thee.'

The dying Christ goes back, as men so often do in the hour and article of death, to the days of his childhood. Aramaic was his mother-tongue, the vernacular of Galilee of the Gentiles. It was in that speech that his mother first recounted to him the wonderful works of God; it was the language of his boyhood and youth; and it is in that dialect that he utters his dying appeal to the God of the old time.

Speaking after the manner of men, may we not say that there was an edge of remonstrance in this prayer? God, however, permits his people to take liberties with him. Asaph, stung with the injustice which he sees on every hand, declares: 'Verily, I have cleansed my heart in vain.' 'Why art thou so far from me, O my God?' complains another afflicted saint. Another enters this resolution upon his tablets: 'I will say unto God my rock, why hast thou forgotten me?' Many others bring their complaints and challenges to the foot of the Throne; and God is willing to have it so, if they come before the righteous Judge with reverent faith, to supplicate justice.

Almost the next word which Jesus utters is the sacred Name 'Father'. The sin of mankind no longer veils the face of Love from the suffering Son. And now, listen!

'IT IS FINISHED!'

CHAPTER FOURTEEN

'INTO THY HANDS I COMMEND MY SPIRIT'
(Luke 23:46)

'And when Jesus had cried with a loud voice, he said, Father, into thy hands I commend my Spirit: and having said this he gave up the ghost'.

After the tense silence that held the watchers round the Cross had been broken by the shout of victory, our Lord surrendered his life as a sacrificial offering to God. The darkness of forsakenness has passed. The comfort of the Father's presence in love and power has been renewed, and faith returns to the joy of full assurance. The prayer which was the instrument of the dismissal of the soul of Jesus from the body of his humiliation was in its original use a cry of distress on the part of one who, 'worn out in mind and body, despised, defamed, and persecuted... casts himself upon God' (Psalm 31).

There are, however, two points of difference between its application to the need of the Psalmist and its employment by the dying Christ: the Psalmist invokes the name of Jehovah, God of the Covenant, and adds to his prayer this argument: 'Thou hast redeemed me.'

Jesus calls upon his Father, and dies on the merit of his own work of redemption.

In the Psalter these words are found in connection, not with the laying down of life, but with the distresses and deliverances of this mortal life. We may be sure that our Lord often applied them to this current use before he appropriated them to be the watchword of his passage from earth to the skies. As he was about to die, so he had lived, committing himself in every hour of trial to the loving care of his Father in heaven. It was, therefore, most natural that he should quote this formula in the article of death.

'Father,' the first recorded utterance of Jesus, and the last, is the sum of the disclosure of the Divine Name which the Saviour came to earth to declare: it is the revelation of Jesus Christ which God gave unto him, to show unto his servants. God is the Father of our Lord Jesus Christ, and, by the grace of the Incarnation, our Father in him. Faith has won its perfect triumph in the utterance of those faltering words. The Man of Sorrows and the Acquainted with Grief, with the dew of Gethsemane's agony upon his brow and the sin of a lost world upon his soul, lays his bruised but victorious life in the hands of infinite love and measureless power, the hands of his Father. Herein is faith made perfect.

May we not see in these words also an assertion of the voluntariness of our Redeemer's

death? He is not overborne in dying forced by a
mightier hand into the dust of death. He lays his
life down of himself, no man taking it from him.
He submits to death, not because he is under
constraint to obey its behests, but because he has
come to do his Father's will: 'This commandment,' he says, 'received I from my Father.' To
him death was not a return to kindred dust, but
an entrance into the Father's house.

In his eventful journey, by water and by blood,
the Redeemer of men has now reached the
golden gates: the Father comes forth to welcome
him. 'Now come I to thee,' he says: and in the
power of his own blood he enters the everlasting
habitations. Our Saviour does not propose to
hasten his own departure, nor will he suffer his
life to be taken from the earth by hostile powers;
dying, he places his soul with unshaken confidence within the clasp of his Father's sheltering
hand.

These words tell us that the redemptive work
of the Saviour is completed. The mightiest work
ever engaged in on this earth was undertaken in
the name of the Holy Trinity by the Incarnate
Son. He came to reconcile the world to God, to
effect an agreement in a disordered creation
between mercy and truth, to accomplish the
salvation of the lost, to break the tyranny of evil
powers, to despoil sin of its unrighteous dominion, to procure for the ungodly the ministration

of the Holy Spirit, and to open the doors of his Father's house to wanderers returning from the land of famine. In bringing these things to pass he endured to the uttermost the sorrows of our mortal state, the contradiction of sinners against himself, the stroke of God's afflictive justice. And now 'it is finished': his travail and his toil are ended.

> Tis finished - was his latest voice;
> These sacred accents o'er,
> He bowed his head, gave up the ghost,
> And suffered pain no more.

> 'Tis finished - the Messiah dies
> For sins, but not his own;
> The great redemption is complete,
> And Satan's power o'erthrown.

Therefore we may pray, as the Psalmist did many centuries ago. When the sorrows of death compass us and the pains of hell lay hold upon us; when our sins, like a pack of wolves, are in full cry after our soul; then may we flee unto God our refuge, saying:

'Into thine hand I commend my spirit: Thou hast redeemed me, O Lord, thou God of truth' (Psalm 31:5)

In this last prayer of his earthly life our Lord has taught us how to die. In all generations the cry of the departing Saviour has rung out as a challenge before the everlasting doors. 'The many instances on record,' says one, 'including St Polycarp, St Basil, Epiphanius of Pavia, St Bernard, St Louis, Huss, Columbus, Luther and Melanchthon - of Christians using these words at the approach of death, represent many millions of unrecorded cases.' The Lord gave the word, great was the company of those who published it.

Was there not also in this prayer of the departing Christ an announcement of his ascent from humiliation to exaltation? He dismissed his spirit; it took its flight to the shelter of the eternal love, the radiance of the unshadowed glory; henceforth it dwells, far from the distances and darkness of this earthly life in the Bosom of God. At times our Lord had seemed to anticipate this hour with intense longing:

'O faithless and perverse generation, how long shall I be with you, and suffer you?' (Luke 9:41)

'I came to cast fire upon the earth, and what will I, if it is already kindled? But I have a baptism to be baptized with; and how am I straitened till it be accomplished' (Luke 12: 49-50)

'And now I am no more in the world, but these are in the world, and I come to thee (John 17)'

The Man of Sorrows is anointed with the oil of gladness above his fellows, the Pilgrim Christ reenters his Father's house, the Lamb that was slain is seated in the midst of the throne, crowned with that radiancy of love which was his before the foundation of the world.

CHAPTER FIFTEEN

'HE EVER LIVETH TO MAKE INTERCESSION'

When the forty days of our Lord's risen life on earth were ended, 'He led them out until they were over against Bethany: and he lifted up his hands, and blessed them. And it came to pass, while he blessed them, he parted from them, and was carried up into heaven' (Luke 24:50, 51). This farewell benediction was the signal of the Redeemer's entrance on his ministry of intercession: the nail-pierced hands, are to us the symbol of his unchangeable priesthood, and the assurance that he ever liveth to make intercession for us.

The heavenly ministry of Christ was foreshadowed in his High-Priestly Prayer. The words 'I pray' do not imply entreaty, but a request as between equals, and this idea is strengthened by the use of the phrase 'I will' (see John 17: 9, 15, 20, 24). Our Lord is no longer the lowly suppliant of earth, wearing the servant's girdle, and perfecting his obedience even unto death (Phil 2:7,8), but the Man who is Jehovah's Fellow. He intercedes from the throne; he offers his requests in the power of an accepted sacrifice; he asks for that purchased possession which is his by right.

It is in the office of Mediator that the Lord Jesus presents his petitions to the Father.

'There is one God, one Mediator also between God and men, Christ Jesus, himself man' (1 Tim 2:5).

To this high function the Messiah has been appointed of old in the eternal covenant. It is his place to make reconciliation between a righteous Judge and sinners of mankind; it is his right to redeem. St John, with the piercing theological insight which characterises his First Epistle, sets forth this mediatorial ministry in all its fullness:

'We have an Advocate with the Father, Jesus Christ the righteous: and he is the propitiation for our sins; and not for ours only, but also for the whole world' (1 John 2:1,2).

Our Saviour mediates on the ground of his finished work - because he has expiated our sins; nay, more, because he is the Expiator, bearing in wounded hands and feet, and brow, and side the assurance that all which could hinder our approach to God has been taken away. It is in the power of his blood that he pleads. And justice is, in him, and for his sake, so strongly enlisted in our favour and defence, that 'Jesus Christ the Righteous' presents the claim of his own righteousness in such wise that it shall have authority with 'the Father' confirming and energising the tender love of him who gave his Son to the death on our behalf.

And how willing that Father is to respond to the righteous plea of the Well-beloved, a saying of the Lord Jesus himself makes manifest:

'In that day ye shall ask in my name: and I say not unto you, that I will make request of the Father for you; for the Father himself loveth you' (John 16:26,27).

Our prayers, ascending in the name of the Lord Jesus, are taken up into his intercession, being presented by him before the throne, with all authority, as if the prayers were his alone; but, says he, there is more than this. It is not only that I shall make intercession for you, precious as that assurance is, but the Father's love is already eagerly anticipating those requests, that he may fulfil all your desires and bestow upon you every good and perfect gift: 'The Father himself loveth you.' And it is of this that the Saviour would have his people think, even more than of his advocacy for them. Few things could pain our Master more than that, in remembering him, we should forget the Father who is the Fountain of God-head love.

It would be idle to ask what form this heavenly

advocacy assumes. The writer of the Epistle to the Hebrews passes beyond all forms to the undying essence:

'For Christ entered not into a holy place made with hands, like in pattern to the true; but into heaven itself, now to appear before the face of God for us' (Heb 9:24).

Our High Priest, having offered himself, now presents himself in the power of a risen life before God on our behalf. As he himself is the propitiation, so he himself is the availing intercession. St John has put this thought into glowing imagery. When the challenge of the strong angel sounded through earth and heaven: 'Who is worthy to open the book, and to loose the seals thereof?' a Lamb, as it had been slain - our Lord, coming up from the conflict and agony of his passion - advanced to the throne, and took the book of the world's guidance out of the hand of him that liveth for ever and ever. Then all the choirs of heaven raised the new song of victorious love:

'Thou art worthy to take the book, and to open the seals thereof: for thou was slain, and didst purchase unto God with thy blood men of every tribe and tongue, and people, and nation' (Rev 5).

It is in the Epistle to the Hebrews that our

Lord's heavenly ministry is most clearly set forth. A verse which throws a flood of light upon the importance of this priestly action of the risen Lord is:

'He, because he abideth for ever, hath his priest-hood unchangeable. Wherefore also he is able to save to the uttermost them that draw near unto God through him, seeing he ever liveth to make intercession for them' (Heb 7:24,25).

He lives to intercede. This is the sum of all his priestly activities in the heavens. From his inter-cession flow the donation of the Spirit and the ministration of spiritual gifts, the growth of grace in the lives of the redeemed, and all the sanctify-ing influences which proceed from the Father's providential care and the mediatorial ministry of the Redeemer.

Let us mention one or two of the fruits of our Saviour's intercession.

(a) It secures to us peace of conscience, and the assurance of the Father's free and unalter-able forgiveness:

'Who is he that shall condemn? It is Christ that died, yea rather, that was raised from the dead, who is at the right hand of God, who also maketh intercession for us' (Rom 8:34).

(b) It provides for our complete sanctification. In a text already quoted we read: 'He is able
to save to the uttermost' - this in the power of his
intercession. Not only *from the uttermost* - that,
thank God, he is able to do - but *to the uttermost*;
piercing to the thoughts and intents of the heart,
reaching to the springs of feeling and desire, and
presenting us faultless before the Father.

(c) In several passages in the Old Testament
the Messiah is represented as leading the worship of Israel. Our Lord seems to accept this view
of his heavenly ministry, as when he says:

'Where two or three are gathered together in my
name, there am I in the midst of them' (Matt
18:20).

One may well believe that our Lord in his
intercession is continually ministering grace
through all the ordinances of the Church.

In a word, the exalted Saviour is fulfilling the
command of his Father:

'Ask of me, and I will give thee the nations for
thine inheritance, and the uttermost parts of the
earth for thy possession' (Psalm 2:8).

He is praying, as he has taught us to pray, for
the coming of that time when the kingdoms of
this world shall become the Kingdom of our

Lord and of his Christ, when Jehovah shall be Ruler over all the earth, when there shall be one Lord, and his Name one. From henceforth he is 'expecting' until all shall do him reverence.